alpha
books

THE
COMPLETE
IDIOT'S
GUIDE TO

Cool Jobs
for *Teens*

by Susan Ireland

A member of Penguin Group (USA) Inc.

This book is dedicated to my oldest brother, Russ, who began working in our family's hotel at the age of 12. His enthusiasm and curiosity led him to try almost every position in the business, from bellhop to chef. I'm grateful that he set this example for his four siblings, and for his support as I wrote this book.

Copyright © 2001 by Susan Ireland

THE COMPLETE IDIOT'S GUIDE TO and Design are registered trademarks of Penguin Group (USA) Inc.

International Standard Book Number: 0-02-864032-2
Library of Congress Catalog Card Number: Available upon request.

07 06 05   8 7 6 5 4

Interpretation of the printing code: The rightmost number of the first series of numbers is the year of the book's printing; the rightmost number of the second series of numbers is the number of the book's printing. For example, a printing code of 01-1 shows that the first printing occurred in 2001.

Printed in the United States of America

Note: This publication contains the opinions and ideas of its author. It is intended to provide helpful and informative material on the subject matter covered. It is sold with the understanding that the author and publisher are not engaged in rendering professional services in the book. If the reader requires personal assistance or advice, a competent professional should be consulted.

Publisher
Marie Butler-Knight

Product Manager
Phil Kitchel

Managing Editor
Jennifer Chisholm

Senior Acquisitions Editor
Randy Ladenheim-Gil

Development Editor
Lynn Northrup

Production Editors
JoAnna Kremer
Christy Wagner

Copy Editor
Susan Aufheimer

Illustrator
Jody Schaeffer

Cover Designer
Dan Armstrong

Book Designer
Gary Adair

Indexer
Angie Bess

Layout/Proofreading
Angela Calvert
John Etchison
Gloria Schurick

Contents at a Glance

Contents

Introduction

You're psyched! Summer's coming and you're going to get a cool job, make some bucks, and have a good time. Okay, maybe you've picked up this book in the dead of winter because you need to get an after-school or weekend job to pay your bills. In either case, what kind of job will you be happy with, and how the heck will you find it?

Getting a job isn't all that hard. There are millions of jobs available, many of which you're qualified to fill. And employers are hungry for a young worker like you who's eager to learn, willing to work relatively cheap, and can adjust to a company's work style.

How This Book Is Organized

Before you jump headlong into the guts of this book, let's look at how it's put together and where you'll find what you need.

Part 1, "Get a Life, Get a Job," is where you'll take a few personality and skill tests to discover what sort of job you're best suited for. Did you just start shaking at the mention of "tests"? Relax. You can't possibly fail these tests, and you may even get a chuckle out of them.

Part 2, "Top Fifty Jobs," is a treasure trove of 50 detailed job descriptions that you can examine to see what each job entails, what skills are required, where you might find such a job opening, and what type of career it could lead to.

Part 3, "Nailing Down the Job," explains the nuts and bolts of getting a job. You'll learn how to find out what jobs are available, how to write a dynamite resume and cover letter, how to fill out an application form, and how to conduct an excellent interview.

Part 4, "You're Hired!" tells you what to expect once you're hired. It explains what tax and governmental stuff you have to comply with as an employee, and how to manage those big bucks that will be coming your way.

Part 5, "Outside the Job Box," gives insight into non-traditional job options such as volunteer positions, internships, and self-employment. You'll discover how these work options are defined, how to get them, and what benefits you're apt to realize.

In addition, you'll find two helpful appendixes: "Agencies That Work" (a listing of state employment agencies) and "Cool Books and Web Sites" (other helpful resources).

Cool Extras

Throughout this book there are four types of sidebars, each containing a warning, piece of advice, resource, or quote. Here's what you'll find:

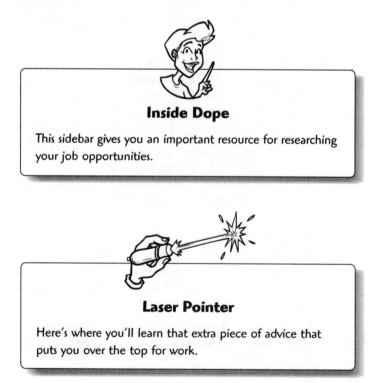

Inside Dope

This sidebar gives you an important resource for researching your job opportunities.

Laser Pointer

Here's where you'll learn that extra piece of advice that puts you over the top for work.

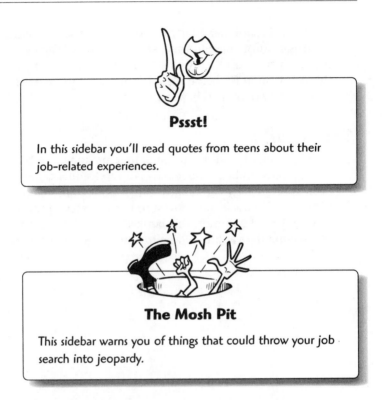

Pssst!

In this sidebar you'll read quotes from teens about their job-related experiences.

The Mosh Pit

This sidebar warns you of things that could throw your job search into jeopardy.

This book is your guide through the employment world. Because many of the tips found between these covers will be useful throughout your career, you should keep this book handy even after you get your first job.

Now it's time to get to work: Let's go find you a cool job!

Acknowledgments

Special thanks to Charlie Vincent, who shared his humor, love, and patience as I wrote this book. My gratitude also goes to Lynn Northrup, Deb Habas, and Goeffrey Welchman for their editorial support; along with Susan, John, Carol, and Rose Habas, and Sam Vincent for their contributions. Nothing in my writing career gets done without the hard work of my literary agent Andrée Abecassis, for which I thank her. Many thanks go to Randy Ladenheim-Gil, Susan Aufheimer, JoAnna Kremer, Christy Wagner, and the production team at Alpha Books. Most important, I thank my mom for being there for me through my years as a young worker and beyond.

Trademarks

All terms mentioned in this book that are known to be or are suspected of being trademarks or service marks have been appropriately capitalized. Alpha Books and Penguin Group (USA) Inc. cannot attest to the accuracy of this information. Use of a term in this book should not be regarded as affecting the validity of any trademark or service mark.

Part 1

Get a Life, Get a Job

You're off to get a job. Where? Oh, you don't have a clue? Then sit down a minute and read this part. Before you can take even one step toward finding your job, you need to figure out what kind of work you want. Now that's going to take a little thinking, but don't worry, I'm here to help you.

As you read through these first two chapters, you may be surprised to learn that holding down a job doesn't necessarily mean a major change to your lifestyle. It's very likely that your job will involve some aspect of your current life—a sport you're good at, an interest you love, a social cause you're hot about, or even a school subject you're crazy about. So go ahead, turn the page, and see what your interests, passions, skills, and drives are telling you to do for work.

Chapter 1

What's So Cool About Having a Job?

In This Chapter

✧ Figuring out if you really want a job

✧ How earning your own money helps you declare your independence

✧ Knowing how to look good on the job no matter what the dress code

✧ Collecting employer references for future jobs

✧ Using short-term jobs to check out a career

There are three answers to the question at the top of this page: swag, swag, and more swag. What is swag, you ask? It's goodies, stuff, loot, spoils, profits, or, as pirates used to say, "booty." (No, not that kind!)

Pirate swag was come by illegally (they stole it). But in the context of your job, swag can mean stuff that you get for making an honest effort.

Swag is what this chapter's about. We're going to talk about the benefits you'll get from holding down a job. Well, what are we waiting for? Let's talk swag!

So, You Want a Job

Do you fall asleep when your parents and teachers talk about your "Few-Cher"? Well wake up, 'cause your job and the task of finding it can be a really cool adventure.

Your first job is an important step, there's no denying it. It's your official introduction to the world of responsibility. When you sign up for a position, you essentially agree to ...

◇ Show up on time.

◇ Keep commitments.

◇ Be honest.

◇ Dress appropriately.

◇ Make your best effort at performing the job.

Here's the cool part: The better you are at doing those five things, the more swag (money and perks) you walk away with. That can be an awesome experience, especially if you enjoy the job. And why work at a job you hate?

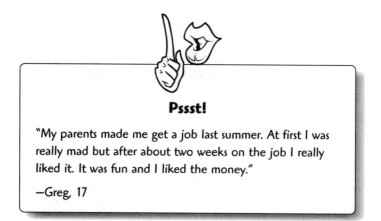

Pssst!

"My parents made me get a job last summer. At first I was really mad but after about two weeks on the job I really liked it. It was fun and I liked the money."

—Greg, 17

Before you plunge headlong into your job search, let's do a reality check to be sure you really *want* a job. Take a stab at this quiz and see what it tells you. Just check Yes or No for each question.

Do You *Really* Want a Job?

1. Does the idea of having a wad of bills in your fist make you do an ecstatic 360?
   ◉ Yes   ○ No

2. Do you want a sure-fire excuse to get away from your parents for a few hours?
   ◉ Yes   ○ No

3. Are your friends all getting summer jobs while you haven't thought past what's next on MTV?
   ○ Yes   ◉ No

4. Do you like to "EXPRESS" yourself by dressing cool and being noticed by people around you?
   ◉ Yes   ○ No

5. Do you wish you could get paid to do something you already love to do?
   ◉ Yes   ○ No

6. Do you quake at the thought of not being able to afford to buy a car, much less pay for the insurance on it?
   ○ Yes   ○ No

7. Do you feel your talents are often underappreciated and you want a chance to prove how good you are?
   ◉ Yes   ○ No

8. Do you ever imagine what good things your first employer will say about you when you apply for your next job?
   ◉ Yes   ○ No

9. Do you have a vague idea of what you might like to do in the future, and would you like a way to test it out?
   ◉ Yes   ○ No

10. Wouldn't you feel kind of proud to be able to grumble to your friends that you have to be at work?
    ◉ Yes   ○ No

If the answer to any or all of the above is "Duh," then read on! We're going to talk about how work can pay off for you.

Mo' Money

You probably already have some money—maybe you get an allowance, you sell your old CDs at garage sales, or you do some chores around the house to pick up a few bucks. But you could always use more, right?

Inside Dope

Read *Opportunities in Part-Time and Summer Jobs* by Adrian A. Pardis (see Appendix B, "Cool Books and Web Sites") to learn what kids got paid in different parts of the country for a number of different jobs.

Getting a job is an obvious way to put more money in your pocket—whether it's to get those new in-lines you want, to buy some hot DVDs, to save money for college, or to put down your first payment toward a root canal (just kidding). Whatever the reason, getting a job will make it possible for you to get the things you want without having to beg your parents for a handout. Isn't that reason enough?

Having your own income will give you much of the independence you're shooting for. When you're bringing in the bucks, no one can tell you how much to spend on those sunglasses you've been lusting over. And if you have a steady stream, you'll be able to afford car payments *and* put gas in the tank. Now you're talking "wheel" independence. Yup, earning money is a good move on your part.

Having Fun at Work

Surprise! Going to work can be one of the high points of your life. Why? Depending on what you do, you could be ...

1. Learning fascinating stuff.

2. Having fun with co-workers.

3. Meeting all kinds of people.

When asked what kids want—aside from money—in a job, most say being with other cool kids is high on the list. They want to make friends; they want to have a good time.

With a few exceptions, the jobs listed in Part 2, "Top Fifty Jobs," involve working with people. But the age and number of co-workers and customers you'd work with depend on the job. Each work environment has its own culture, which in turn tends to attract customers and employees who fit into that culture.

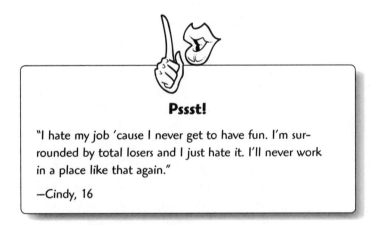

Pssst!

"I hate my job 'cause I never get to have fun. I'm surrounded by total losers and I just hate it. I'll never work in a place like that again."

—Cindy, 16

For instance, if you worked as a sales associate in the kitchenware department of a busy store in downtown Manhattan, your fellow employees would probably be women, 20 years old and older. On an average day, you might serve as many as 150 customers, mostly women 25 years and older. Before taking that job, you'd want to ask yourself if those are the people you want to work with and wait on every day. If your answer is "yes," then go for the job. But if you think you wouldn't be at ease with that group of people, look for work somewhere else.

To make sure you end up working with the kinds of people you enjoy, answer the following questions:

1. How much do you want to be with people on the job? Do you want constant interaction or just an occasional "hi" with a co-worker?

2. Is there a particular age group you want to be with? Do you want to work with children, kids your age, middle-aged people, or the elderly?

3. Would you be content to work with the same people each day, or do you want more variety? For example, would you get tired of seeing the same faces each day in a small organization or would you prefer to work with the general public where you'd rub elbows with many different people?

4. Do you want to be able to joke around a lot on the job or are you looking for a more sedate work environment?

The answers to these questions could help you spot the right workplace for you. Keep them in mind as you do your job search.

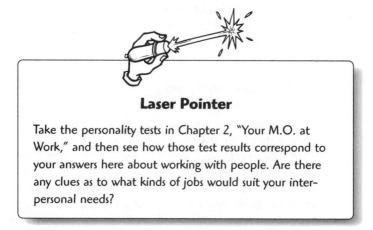

Laser Pointer

Take the personality tests in Chapter 2, "Your M.O. at Work," and then see how those test results correspond to your answers here about working with people. Are there any clues as to what kinds of jobs would suit your inter-personal needs?

Looking Good on the Job

Every day you go to work, chances are you'll get to search through your closet to come up with a cool outfit to wear. One day you may wear your new khakis to impress a co-worker; another day you may dress up a little since you know the boss wants to talk to you about a raise.

Sure, some jobs (like waiting tables or working in a hospital) require a uniform, but even in those jobs there's usually room for a personal touch—shoes, jewelry (limited in most cases), how you do your hair, what you carry your stuff in (backpack or purse). If you're like me, you may have a few "Gaps" in your fashion sense. Don't worry. Just start checking out some of those people at the mall who seem to pull it off.

Even if the fashion police aren't patrolling your company, have fun with your clothes and accessories. Looking appropriately cool will make you feel good, and that will help you do a good job. But while it's great to express your individuality and show the world how cool you are, don't go overboard and wear something that could be a distraction, like a belly shirt that's cut up to *there* or that T-shirt with the four-letter words on it. No matter how sharp you think it looks, remember that you're representing the company. You want to look like you've got it under control! Some other things to avoid (unless you're sure they match the company's image) include ...

- ✧ Those cool low-rider pants that show off your navel ring.
- ✧ Ripped, torn, or dirty anything.
- ✧ Tank tops (for guys or girls).
- ✧ That big dangly pair of earrings.
- ✧ Your blue glitter hair gel.
- ✧ Slathering yourself in cologne or after-shave.
- ✧ Too much makeup on girls, or any makeup on guys.

It Feels Good to ...

You know the feeling that comes from a hard workout or finally getting that English paper turned in? How about the satisfaction you get when you place in the 100-meter run?

A good day at work can have the same sort of rewards. Whether your job is physically or mentally demanding, you can get off work feeling proud of what you've accomplished. You'll find that doing a job well can ...

⬧ Boost your self-image.

⬧ Give you more confidence.

⬧ Prepare you for working as part of a team.

⬧ Help you learn how to go after things you want.

These four points are really important to being happy on the job. That's why it's worth investing the concentration and effort it takes to do your job the best you can.

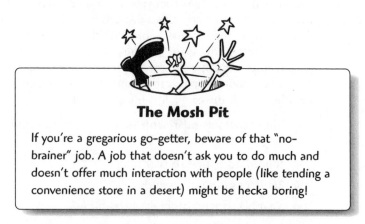

The Mosh Pit

If you're a gregarious go-getter, beware of that "no-brainer" job. A job that doesn't ask you to do much and doesn't offer much interaction with people (like tending a convenience store in a desert) might be hecka boring!

For Future Reference

Every time you hold a job, especially when you do well at it, your boss can become a reference for future employers. In other words, when you apply for your second job, your potential employer may want to call your first employer to ask him or her what kind of a worker you were.

With every job you take, this list will become impressively longer. So, starting with your first job, you're building toward your next job, and the next, and ultimately toward your career.

To have that list of references when you need it, you have to do a little footwork. Before your last day on a job (say, at the end of your summer job or when you decide to move from one after-school job to another), follow the working dude's (or dudette's) three R's: Record, Reference, and Recommendation.

Let's see what's entailed in each of these R's.

Record

Keep a record of each job that you hold. To make that task easy, use this handy form.

Your Employment Record

Name of the organization where you worked:

_____

Mailing address of the organization:

_____

E-mail address of the organization:

_____

Date you started working there:

_____

Date you left your job there:

_____

Name of your supervisor:

_____

Your supervisor's phone number:

_____

Your job title:

_____

Short description of your job:

_____

_____

_____

What you liked best about your job:

_____

_____

_____

What you didn't like:

_____

_____

_____

Fill out one of these forms every time you leave a job and put the form into a file folder or big envelope. Keep that packet in a safe place where you can find it next summer or whenever you start looking for another job and you need to dig up your former employment info.

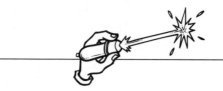

Laser Pointer

Before you fill out this form, make some copies of it so that you'll have them for several jobs down the road.

Reference

Before your last day on the job, ask your employer for permission to use him as a reference for future job applications.

Then, when it comes time to give out a reference to another employer, call your former boss to get the most up-to-date address and phone number and to let him know you're about to give out contact info to a prospective employer. That way, your former boss won't be surprised to get a call about you ("Who the heck is Robyn Ublind?").

When you call your former boss to say that you're about to use him as a reference in your job search, begin by reminding your boss who you are. For example, "Hello Mr. Buckland, I'm Robyn Ublind. I worked in your accounting department last summer." Your boss will appreciate the memory tickler and will also recall what a fantastic worker you were.

Then go on to explain that a potential employer might be calling. ("You once told me that you would be a reference for me. I just want to let you know that I've given your name to Mr. Payback at Dewey, Cheatem & Howe where I'm applying for a part-time position.")

Recommendation

Before your last day on the job (and once you're sure your boss knows that you're leaving), ask your boss to write you a short letter of recommendation stating what position you held and what your strengths were as an employee. This letter is good to have whether or not you're getting another job immediately. To see what a letter of recommendation looks like, check out the sample on the next page.

If your employer hems and haws when you ask for a letter of recommendation, offer to draft the letter yourself. Then ask your boss to put it on the company stationery, make any necessary changes, and sign it. A letter of recommendation is a valuable thing to have, even if you have to turn a few cartwheels to get it (like writing the letter on your boss's behalf and giving it to him on a diskette so that it can be downloaded onto a computer). You've worked hard and you deserve the consideration of your boss's written appreciation. After all, a good letter of recommendation could help you land a better job next time, and that could be worth a lot!

The Mosh Pit

Don't ask your employer for a letter of recommendation when he is all stressed out. If your boss is in a frenzy over something, wait until later when your boss isn't so busy and when writing a letter won't seem like such a big deal.

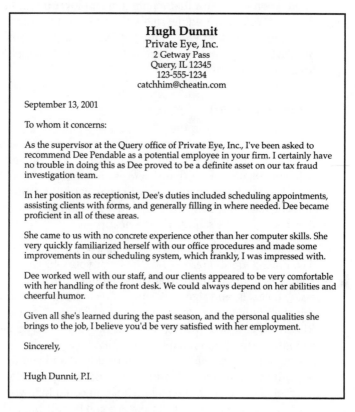

Hugh Dunnit
Private Eye, Inc.
2 Getway Pass
Query, IL 12345
123-555-1234
catchhim@cheatin.com

September 13, 2001

To whom it concerns:

As the supervisor at the Query office of Private Eye, Inc., I've been asked to recommend Dee Pendable as a potential employee in your firm. I certainly have no trouble in doing this as Dee proved to be a definite asset on our tax fraud investigation team.

In her position as receptionist, Dee's duties included scheduling appointments, assisting clients with forms, and generally filling in where needed. Dee became proficient in all of these areas.

She came to us with no concrete experience other than her computer skills. She very quickly familiarized herself with our office procedures and made some improvements in our scheduling system, which frankly, I was impressed with.

Dee worked well with our staff, and our clients appeared to be very comfortable with her handling of the front desk. We could always depend on her abilities and cheerful humor.

Given all she's learned during the past season, and the personal qualities she brings to the job, I believe you'd be very satisfied with her employment.

Sincerely,

Hugh Dunnit, P.I.

Sample letter of recommendation.

Getting Your Career Feet Wet

Short-term and part-time jobs can be a wonderful way to "try on" a particular type of work you think you might want to pursue as a career. For instance, if you've always thought you might want to own a restaurant someday, working as a server or short-order cook would be a great way to find out if, in fact, you really like that kind of work. Or maybe you think you'd like to be a child psychologist after you graduate from college. Working in a daycare center all summer might tell you whether or not you really want a career dealing with kids and their parents.

Get the picture? Your summer or after-school job can be an experiment for bigger things to come. If the experiment goes well, you can soar ahead with academic and career plans. If it goes sour, you've got plenty of time to check out other career options.

Laser Pointer

Look through the job descriptions in Part 2 to see if any of them sound like something that might lead to your career.

Job Smarts That Last a Lifetime

Getting a summer or after-school job accomplishes a few things. In addition to making your own money, you're going to develop skills that will help in your "Few-Cher." These will include (don't worry, it won't be as bad as eating Brussels sprouts) …

1. Discovering what kind of work you'll be happy doing.

2. Finding a workplace that suits your personality.

3. Learning how to get along with all kinds of people.

4. Applying for and getting the job even when there's lots of competition.

5. Negotiating a good pay rate.

6. Managing your money so you can live the way you want to.

Here's something you already know: Practice makes ... you better at something. You don't learn unless you practice, whether you want to play guitar, shoot hoops, or write a new computer program. The more you work at something, the easier it becomes ... even the job of finding work!

Inside Dope

Join the job forum with other first-time workers at www.studentcenter.org/forum. At this site you can post topics, respond to others' questions, and tell the world what you're thinking about job-wise.

If this is your first job, you may feel a little intimidated about putting yourself out there. It may take a few applications before you find yourself employed. But every time you go on an interview, every time you fill out a job application form, every time you even ask if there's a job opening, you're going to do it more smoothly and with more finesse.

Before long you'll be a pro at landing a job that puts cash in your pocket, teaches you valuable skills, gives you a chance to make friends and have fun, and maybe even leads to an exciting career. Not bad swag!

The Least You Need to Know

◈ Earning money can give you a sense of independence, and can help you achieve your material, social, and educational goals.

◈ On the job, you'll make friends and, depending on the type of business, interact with lots of different people who are your customers.

◈ Every day is a chance to look cool by wearing the right kind of clothes and accessories.

◈ Working hard on the job can give you a lot of satisfaction.

◈ Each job you take is an opportunity to put one more employer on your list of references.

◈ A summer or after-school job might be a chance to discover your dream career.

Chapter 2

Your M.O.
at Work

In This Chapter

✧ Finding work that matches your skills, interests, and personality

✧ Getting the 411 on a job

✧ What's up with part-time and full-time work

✧ Do you want to be a manager?

We all know one kid who knew she wanted to be a veterinarian since she was five, and who probably *will* be a veterinarian one day because it's *all* she ever wanted to do.

If your M.O. (mode of operation) isn't that clear, don't worry. A lot of us (including me) find our careers by trial and error, which means there's no wrong way to start. Just start. How? By getting a job.

What's important is to find a job that you'll like. This chapter has a few "tests" to help you figure out how your personality, skills, and interests can come together to define your work M.O.

Doing What You Already Do Best

The first step in choosing your job is figuring out what job skills you have. "Hey, wait a sec," you say. "How can I have job skills if I've never had a job?"

It's simple: There are things you've done in your everyday life that could qualify as job skills and could also give you some direction in your job search. For instance ...

✧ If you're good with numbers, you might love mastering the change at a cash register.

✧ If you're outdoorsy and you're not afraid to get your fingernails dirty, you might like to be a park ranger's assistant.

✧ If you're a whiz at fixing computer glitches for friends and family, you might be a natural to work as a tech-support guy (or girl) at your local computer store.

Here's a worksheet you can use to make note of what skills and interests you could turn into a paid job.

Your Job Skills

Which of your skills are you proudest of?

_____

What jobs do you think might use that skill?

1. _____

2. _____

3. _____

What's another skill you love to use?

_____

What jobs do you think might use that skill?

1. _____

2. _____

3. _____

If you had to teach a workshop, what subject would it be in?

_____

What jobs do you think involve that subject?

1. _____

2. _____

3. _____

If you could learn about anything in the world, what would it be?

_____

What jobs do you think involve that subject?

1. _____

2. _____

3. _____

If you feel like cheating on this quiz, go ahead and check the "What it takes" section in each of the job descriptions in Part 2, "Top Fifty Jobs."

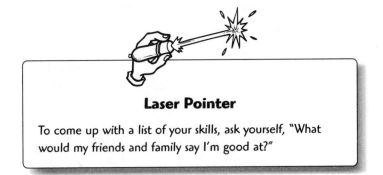

Laser Pointer

To come up with a list of your skills, ask yourself, "What would my friends and family say I'm good at?"

A Test You Can't Fail

To help you get down to the nitty-gritty job-interest-wise, here's a pop quiz (don't worry, you didn't have to study!)

that'll give you insight into your personality and how it can help you in the working world. Just circle the answer that best describes you.

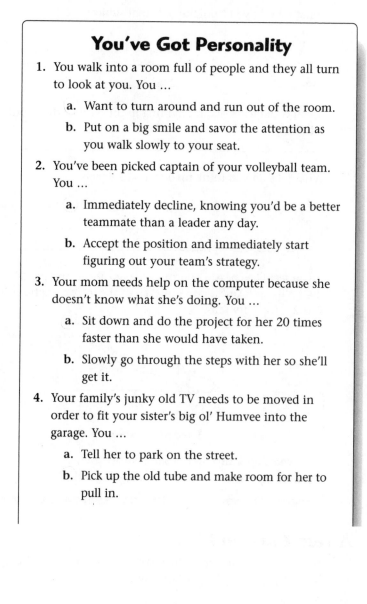

You've Got Personality

1. You walk into a room full of people and they all turn to look at you. You ...

   a. Want to turn around and run out of the room.

   b. Put on a big smile and savor the attention as you walk slowly to your seat.

2. You've been picked captain of your volleyball team. You ...

   a. Immediately decline, knowing you'd be a better teammate than a leader any day.

   b. Accept the position and immediately start figuring out your team's strategy.

3. Your mom needs help on the computer because she doesn't know what she's doing. You ...

   a. Sit down and do the project for her 20 times faster than she would have taken.

   b. Slowly go through the steps with her so she'll get it.

4. Your family's junky old TV needs to be moved in order to fit your sister's big ol' Humvee into the garage. You ...

   a. Tell her to park on the street.

   b. Pick up the old tube and make room for her to pull in.

5. In school you accidentally knock the Bunsen burner off the lab table and it falls into pieces on the floor. You ...

    a. Lay the pieces out carefully on the table and figure out how to put the burner together again.

    b. Figure you'll never be able to put the darn thing back together so you 'fess up and hope you don't have to pay for it.

Now let's see how each of your answers translates into job possibilities.

If you chose **1a**, you're an introvert. Go for support-type positions (Chapter 4), care-giving work with animals (Chapter 5), manual labor (Chapter 6), or skilled specialist jobs (Chapter 7).

If you chose **1b**, you're an extrovert. Consider jobs on the front line of a company (Chapter 3) or care-giving jobs where you work with people (Chapter 5).

The Mosh Pit

Don't go overboard with the quiz results in this chapter. Finding a job is a "gut feel" thing, not a hard science. Use the tests to get you thinking in the right direction.

If you chose **2a**, you're a team player. Look for work in a supporting role (Chapter 4), in care giving (Chapter 3), or in some of the skilled jobs (Chapter 7).

If you chose **2b**, you're a good leader. Start with a front-line position (Chapter 3) for your first job and then reach for a management role in any of the jobs listed in Part 2.

If you chose **3a**, you're a get-things-done kind of person. You'd be great at doing front-line work (Chapter 3), support jobs (Chapter 4), manual labor (Chapter 6), and skilled positions (Chapter 7).

If you chose **3b**, you're a nurturer. Find a job where you can help people or animals (Chapter 5).

If you chose **4a**, you're a tad lazy when it comes to manual work, especially if it might make you sweat. Go for sit-down, front-line jobs (Chapter 3), less physical, supporting positions (Chapter 4), and stationary skilled jobs (Chapter 7).

If you chose **4b**, you like to work hard physically. Try on-your-feet-type jobs on the front line (Chapter 3), physical-work jobs in a supporting role (Chapter 4), some of the more strenuous care-giving jobs (Chapter 5), make-you-sweat jobs (Chapter 6), and physically demanding skilled jobs (Chapter 7).

Inside Dope

To take more thorough personality and interest tests, check out the following free Web sites: Career Search (cbweb9p. collegeboard.org/career/html/searchQues.html) and The Career Interests Game (web.missouri.edu/~cppcwww/ holland.shtml/).

If you chose **5a**, you're a precise person who enjoys solving problems. Think about doing manual work (Chapter 6) or skilled jobs (Chapter 7).

If you chose **5b**, you've not mechanically inclined. Go for a front-line job (Chapter 3) or a care-giving job (Chapter 5).

Taking Leads from School

Another way to figure out what you like doing is to think about your favorite school subjects (and, no, lunch is not a subject). The subjects you actually like to learn about could point to certain kinds of jobs (such as ... biology? Ever thought about working at a pet store or a water treatment plant?). Use this worksheet to rank your school subjects.

What's Your Subject?

What are your favorite classes? Prioritize your list so number one is your favorite.

1. _____
2. _____
3. _____

What classes do you get the best grades in?

1. _____
2. _____
3. _____

What classes do you wish you could do better in and would like to learn more about outside of school?

1. _____
2. _____
3. _____

Inside Dope

The U.S. Bureau of Labor Statistics has a cool Web site (stats.bls.gov/k12/html/edu_over.htm) that explains what careers could come from doing well in certain school subjects.

Did one or two of your subjects appear as an answer to all three of these questions? If so, look at the following lists to see what sort of job that subject might lead you to.

Social Studies

Baby-sitter (Chapter 5)

Child-care worker (Chapter 5)

Dispatcher (Chapter 4)

Fast-food worker (Chapter 3)

Food counter attendant (Chapter 3)

Home companion (Chapter 5)

Hotel or motel desk clerk (Chapter 3)

Maid (Chapter 4)

Receptionist (Chapter 3)

Restaurant host or hostess (Chapter 3)

Retail salesperson (Chapter 3)

Waitperson (Chapter 3)

Science

Cook (Chapter 7)

Fruit and vegetable picker (Chapter 6)

Groundskeeper (Chapter 6)

Kitchen helper (Chapter 4)

Landscape worker (Chapter 6)

Nurse's aide (Chapter 5)

Photographic processor (Chapter 7)

Recyclable material collector (Chapter 6)

Veterinary assistant (Chapter 5)

Zookeeper's helper (Chapter 5)

Language Arts

Administrative assistant (Chapter 4)

Administrative support person (Chapter 4)

Library assistant (Chapter 4)

Word processor (Chapter 7)

Math

Bank teller (Chapter 3)

Cashier (Chapter 3)

Computer programmer (Chapter 7)

Data-entry person (Chapter 7)

Mail clerk (Chapter 4)

Music and the Arts

Dog groomer's helper (Chapter 5)

Graphic designer (Chapter 7)

Indoor or outdoor painter (Chapter 7)

Web site designer/developer (Chapter 7)

Laser Pointer

Consider jobs that fall under both your first and second choice school subjects so you won't miss your killer job.

Gym

Amusement park attendant (Chapter 5)

Bellhop (Chapter 6)

Camp counselor (Chapter 5)

Deckhand on a fishing boat (Chapter 6)

Messenger (Chapter 4)

Sports instructor (Chapter 5)

Warehouse worker (Chapter 6)

Tech

Auto service technician (Chapter 7)

Car washer (Chapter 6)

Carpenter's assistant (Chapter 7)

Construction helper (Chapter 6)

Gas station attendant (Chapter 3)

Janitor (Chapter 4)

Printing shop assistant (Chapter 7)

Technical support person (Chapter 4)

Looking back at your last three quizzes, do you see a trend in the type of work that might make you happy? If so, you're ready to move on to the next step: the 411 interview.

Getting the Inside Scoop

Let's say you picked "Tech" as your favorite subject, so you think you'd like to work at an auto shop this summer to learn more about cars. Before you apply for an auto service technician position, you should find out what duties a service tech is expected to do, right?

To get the scoop, you could arrange what we'll call the "411 interview," where you'd talk to someone who works in that line of business and who can explain what's involved in the job. This could be as simple as quizzing your uncle Vinnie, the mechanic, to see what his helper does on a typical day at his shop, or going to another auto shop and asking if you could talk to a mechanic for a few minutes about how he got started as a service tech.

The Mosh Pit

Be prepared for the possible bad news that your dream job *isn't* your dream job after all. Getting the 411 might tell you things that you don't like (for example, it might require that you do one of those dreaded items from this chapter's first quiz). Learning that early gives you time to switch to something you *will* like.

Here are some good questions to ask during the 411 interview:

- ✧ What's a typical day on the job like in this company?
- ✧ What are the skills required for an entry-level job?
- ✧ Generally speaking, what are the starting wages for this type of job?
- ✧ What's your favorite aspect of your job?
- ✧ What are some of the drawbacks of this work?
- ✧ Is there anyone else you recommend I speak with about this type of work?

By the way, it's a good idea to write your questions down and take your list with you to your meeting. That way you won't forget to ask anything.

Although the primary goal of your conversation with Uncle Vinnie or your mechanic friend is to learn about auto shop work, there might be a side benefit: His shop might have an opening for someone like you! Or if not, he might know about an opening at another place. If he doesn't volunteer the name of another place, ask him for one. (Note the last question on the 411 list.)

Part-Time vs. Full-Time

The next step is to decide how much time you want to devote to a job. From topside, there are two categories:

- ✧ Part-time
- ✧ Full-time

A full-time job is a big commitment, even if it's only for two or three summer months. Full-time means you work 28 plus hours a week, usually 5 days out of the week. (There are some age restrictions on working full-time, which I tell you about in Chapter 13, "You, the Law, and the IRS.") Full-time workers often refer to their nine-to-five jobs, which means they start at nine o'clock in the morning and work until five o'clock in the evening, with a half-hour or one-hour break for lunch and a few short breaks in the morning and afternoon. Of course, some companies (like hospitals and radio stations) have 24-hour operations with three eight-hour shifts to allow round-the-clock coverage. In that case, you may find yourself working in the middle of the night (say, 11:00 P.M. to 7:00 A.M.), otherwise known as the "graveyard shift."

A part-time job is any job that's less than 28 hours a week. This could be a small- to medium-sized commitment, whether it's a couple hours every other evening at the local ice cream parlor (eight hours a week) or eight hours a day on weekends (16 hours a week). If you're looking for a job during your school year, you probably want a part-time position.

Pssst!

"I tried to do a job that was four hours a day on school days 'cause I needed the money but it was way too much. I was falling asleep in class and everything. So I quit that job and got one that was only eight hours a day on the weekend."

—Cynthia, 17

Putting It All Together

You've answered a lot of questions in this chapter. Now let's pull all that info together to create a Job M.O. Blueprint for you.

Job M.O. Blueprint

1. What do you want to avoid doing at your next job?

   _____

2. What skills do you have that you might like to use on the job? (See the "Doing What You Already Do Best" section.)

   _____

3. What personality traits do you have that would come in handy on the job? (See the "A Test You Can't Fail" section.)

   _____

4. What school subjects do you like? (See the "Taking Leads from School" section.)

   _____

5. Do you want to work full time or part time? (See the "Part-Time vs. Full-Time" section.)

   _____

There you have it: six points that describe the type of job you're looking for. Now browse through the job descriptions in Part 2 to see which ones fit your M.O.

The Least You Need to Know

✧ Apply for a job that requires skills you already know you have.

✧ A job that suits your interests and personality is one that you're apt to like.

✧ Your job might complement one of your favorite subjects in school, and give you a chance to learn more about that topic.

✧ Get the inside scoop on the job you're curious about by doing a 411 interview with someone in that line of work.

✧ Full-time work is 28 or more hours a week; part-time work is less than 28 hours a week.

Part 2
Top Fifty Jobs

It's time to spread your job cards on the table and pick the ones that suit you. This part of the book contains a bunch of job descriptions, which, like a deck of cards, are laid before you in the next five chapters.

There are two ways to approach this card trick: You can read all 50 of the job descriptions that appear in these chapters or you can examine only the ones that appeal to you. You can also use these chapters for brainstorming: As you read each job description, imagine yourself doing that particular job and decide how you'd like it.

At the end of each chapter, you'll find 10 more job suggestions that fit into that category. And if the 100 jobs mentioned in this part don't get you on track for a job, I'll bet they'll get you in the mood to come up with your own job discovery.

Enough talk—let's turn the page and start choosing your cool job!

Chapter 3

On the Front Line

In This Chapter

❖ Front-line jobs: what they are and where to find them

❖ Using your math skills on the cash register

❖ Looking at possibilities in the food service industry

❖ A great job in store as a salesperson

❖ Jobs that put you behind the desk of a hotel, bank, or front lobby

Do you love chatting it up with strangers in an airport or making people chuckle with a funny comment while standing in line at the supermarket? If so, you can proudly call yourself a people person, which means you'd be good in a front-line job.

This chapter is about front-line jobs that deal directly with customers. That could range from parking Corvettes in a downtown parking garage to serving sunny-side-up eggs to groggy business professionals.

People Who Need People

Because you're reading this chapter, at least one of the following must be true:

1. When you took the "You've Got Personality" quiz in Chapter 2, "Your M.O. at Work," you marked one or more of these answers: 1b, 2a, 2b, 3a, 4a, 4b, and 5b.

2. You enjoy at least one of these classes: social studies, math, or tech. (See the "What's Your Subject?" worksheet in Chapter 2.)

3. You've decided to read all the job descriptions in Part 2, "Top Fifty Jobs," to see if one jumps out at you.

4. You want to pursue a front-line–type career and you're hoping this chapter will point you in that direction.

That being the case, you should definitely read on to learn about these front-line positions:

Cashier	Retail salesperson
Restaurant host or hostess	Receptionist
Waitperson	Hotel desk clerk
Counter attendant	Bank teller
Fast-food worker	Gas station attendant

The Mosh Pit

Don't get depressed that most entry-level jobs pay so little. As you go through these job descriptions, make note of which ones offer perks such as tips, purchase discounts, or rewards, in addition to an hourly wage.

For each of these positions, you can expect to be paid minimum wage or a little more. The actual amount depends upon how much work experience you have, how much the particular employer pays, and what the going rate is in your part of the country.

A Cashier You Can Count On

A cashier is one of the most important front-line positions a business can have. Handling money can be tricky and it takes a highly responsible person to fill the job. If you were a cashier, here's what you'd do:

✧ Total customers' purchases, using a cash register or scanner

✧ Take their cash, check, or credit card

✧ Give them change and a receipt

✧ Answer customers' questions

✧ Count the money in the cash register at the beginning and end of your shift

Aside from dealing with money, cashiers in some businesses package to-go orders (if they're working in a restaurant), calculate exchanges and refunds (if they're working in a retail store), issue frequent-buyer cards, and bag or wrap merchandise for the customer.

Inside Dope

When it gets close to summer, sniff out your favorite teen magazines (like *COSMO girl*, *Seventeen*, and *Teen People*). They're bound to have good articles about what's happening in the summer job market.

What it takes: If you go for this job, be ready to do repetitious work with accuracy. Your basic math skills and dexterity will come in handy, along with your ability to learn how to use equipment such as cash registers, credit card processors, and bar code scanners. Because you'll be representing the company to the public, you'll be asked to dress to match the image of the biz (for instance, a professional outfit if you're a cashier in an upscale boutique or T-shirt and jeans if you're working in a surf shop).

Where the jobs are: Cashiering jobs can be found in any business where there's a cash register. Look for openings at retail stores (such as grocery stores and gift shops), rental outlets (like video stores and places that rent sports equipment), and service businesses (such as restaurants and gas stations).

What this could lead to: If you like working as a cashier, you might consider a career in the financial services industry as a banker, stock broker, insurance agent, financial advisor, or accountant. Or you may enjoy a career as a customer service representative or manager.

Table for Two

Restaurant hosts and hostesses are usually employed at large, busy, or fancy restaurants. They're the ones who ...

✧ Greet customers as they arrive.

✧ Show them to their table.

✧ Assign tables to waiters and waitresses.

✧ Respond to customer questions and resolve complaints.

✧ Answer the phone and make reservations.

Dining room hosts and hostesses don't usually get many tips; however, some places have a tip pooling policy, which means all the tips get split among all the service workers.

The Mosh Pit

Don't fall for the idea that restaurant hosts and hostesses have it easy. There's a lot of responsibility that falls on their shoulders when the lines of hungry customers grow long.

What it takes: This job requires a friendly personality that gives customers the immediate feeling that they've picked the right place to eat. You'll need a good sense of organization to seat customers promptly and distribute the work equally among the waiters and waitresses. Your ability to think fast on your feet will help you resolve unforeseen problems (after all, you'll be in charge of the dining room operations). You'll be expected to wear clothing that distinguishes you as the head of the dining room (that could mean a uniform that's a different color from the wait staff, or a professional getup of some kind).

Where the jobs are: Any busy restaurant will need a host or hostess to handle the traffic. That could be a diner, coffee shop, or fine-dining restaurant. Check your Yellow Pages and newspaper classifieds to find a restaurant you'd have fun working in.

What this could lead to: Hosts and hostesses might eventually move into restaurant management. Other customer-oriented careers include airline attendant, tour guide, travel agent, and hotel reservations manager.

Waiting to Serve You

Waiters and waitresses are essential to every eating establishment that has sit-down service. In short, here's what a waitperson does on the job:

- ✧ Takes customers' food orders and sometimes makes recommendations
- ✧ Serves food and drinks
- ✧ Prepares itemized checks
- ✧ Answers customers' questions about the food

In small restaurants, a waitperson might also escort customers to their tables, set up and clear tables, and act as the cashier. In larger, more upscale places, a waitperson might explain to customers how a dish is prepared or answer other questions about the menu. Above all, a waiter or waitress is someone who tries to make customers happy through efficient service. Waiting on tables is hard work, but filled with lots of rewards including tips and either free or cheap meals.

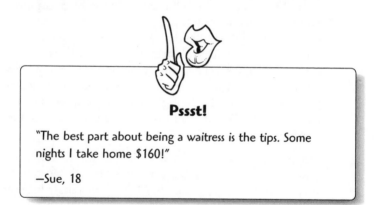

Pssst!

"The best part about being a waitress is the tips. Some nights I take home $160!"

—Sue, 18

What it takes: You must have a good memory for keeping orders straight. The job requires a lot of stamina because you'll be on your feet and carrying trays of food throughout your shift. Basic arithmetic is important for handling bills, making change, and, of course, adding up your tips. You might be required to wear a uniform (picture yourself in Lederhosen with a red apron while working at Fraulein Schnitzel's Hofbrau) or to follow a specific dress code (like black pants and white button-down shirt or blouse at a 1950s-style diner). Most important is your ability to stay upbeat even when dealing with difficult (and hungry) customers.

Where the jobs are: Restaurants, diners, coffee shops, and cafés hire waiters and waitresses. Check the classifieds in the newspaper, respond to Help Wanted signs in restaurant windows, or just ask the manager of an eating establishment if there's a position available.

What this could lead to: Your experience waiting on tables could inspire you to become a chef, restaurant manager, bartender, or food critic. In large chains, good employees are often invited to enter management training programs.

Counter Intelligence

Counter attendants attend customers at counters. (Whoa, was I going too fast for you there?) Seriously, counter attendants work at diners, cafeterias, lunch rooms, coffee shops—anywhere food is being served at a counter. In cafeterias, attendants dish out food that customers put on their trays and take to their tables. Where customers sit at counters (as in coffee shops), counter attendants ...

✧ Take food and drink orders from customers.

✧ Give food orders to the kitchen and pick them up when they're ready.

✧ Serve food.

✧ Prepare itemized checks.

✧ Keep the counter and other areas clean.

✧ Wrap to-go orders.

Depending upon the size of the diner or coffee shop, counter attendants may also prepare some food, such as ice-cream sundaes and sandwiches, or work the cash register. At cafeterias, they might carve meat, ladle soups and sauces, and fill beverage glasses.

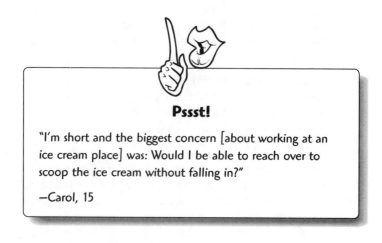

Pssst!

"I'm short and the biggest concern [about working at an ice cream place] was: Would I be able to reach over to scoop the ice cream without falling in?"

—Carol, 15

What it takes: A good disposition is a counter attendant's best friend, since he or she encounters a wide range of personalities who are often in a hurry to get their food. Physical endurance is necessary for standing long hours at a steam table or food stand.

Where the jobs are: You can find work as a counter attendant at cafeterias in schools, corporations, hospitals, and government agencies. Other businesses that offer counter service include diners, coffee shops, ice cream parlors, and cafés.

What this could lead to: Counter attendants who like working in the food industry may become waiters or bartenders. Some may move on to management positions in restaurants and cafeterias.

Want Fries with That?

Fast-food workers perform their magic behind counters and drive-thru windows at familiar places such as McDonald's, Jack in the Box, Wendy's, and your local-yocal burger joint. Here's what fast-food workers typically do:

- ✧ Take food and drink orders from customers
- ✧ Pick up the orders and serve them
- ✧ Tally orders, take payments, and give back change

✧ Cook and package food

✧ Fill beverage cups from drink-dispensing machines

These positions are excellent entry-level jobs because the tasks are simple and the training is good.

What it takes: You just need a willingness to learn. The duties of a fast-food worker aren't difficult, but they require teamwork and a lot of standing and smiling. Remember, this is a front-line job and that means you need to be pleasant to customers and give them good service. And did I mention *fast* service?

Where the jobs are: We all know the names of the big fast-food places where you can apply for a job. Also look into your local drive-thru hangouts to see if they have a summer, after school, or weekend opening.

Inside Dope

For hot leads on cool summer jobs, go to www.summerjobs.com.

What this could lead to: Out of all the fast-food workers, only a small percentage will stay in the fast-food business. Those who do may move into management positions and may eventually own fast-food chain franchises; or they may branch out and start their own full-fledged restaurants.

That's Sales Biz

Retail salespeople (also called sales associates) appear seemingly out of nowhere when you step into a store. They're the ones who offer to help you spend your greenbacks. If you were a sales associate, here's what your job would entail:

✧ Helping customers find what they're looking for in the store

✧ Answering questions about products

✧ Taking payment for merchandise and giving change and receipts

✧ Bagging merchandise for the customer

✧ Handling returns or exchanges

✧ Stocking store shelves or racks

Sales associates work in a wide range of retail outlets from high-end computer stores to nickel-and-dime newsstands. In some stores, the sales associates get commissions (a percentage of the sales) for the items they sell. They may also get discounts on purchases they make in the store. (Wouldn't you like to get 10 percent off the price of your next hard drive?) Some employers also offer rewards (like vacation trips and concert tickets) for individual and team sales achievements (called quotas).

What it takes: Above all, it takes excellent interpersonal skills to do well as a salesperson. Customers often judge a store by its salespeople, so giving courteous service is ultra-important. Your ability to adapt to different personalities, to listen attentively, and to respond to your customers' needs will pay off big time. Knowledge (or willingness to learn) about the store's products is essential to convincing customers to exchange their money for merchandise. And, as always, a neat appearance is bound to impress a potential employer.

Where the jobs are: Retail sales jobs are everywhere that merchandise is sold. If there's a storefront and a product is being sold inside, there might be a sales position available. You may even see signs in those front windows beckoning you inside to fill out an application form.

Laser Pointer

Looking for a retail sales position? Inquire in stores that sell something you know a lot about. For instance, if you're a comic book junky, you might do really well at Marvel Joe's Comic Books where you can talk all day about Wolverine's battles with Magneto.

What this could lead to: Salespeople may go on to become store managers, or use their skills to open their own stores. Or, they may become manufacturer's sales representatives (also called sales reps) or distributors who sell products wholesale to stores.

Lip Service

A receptionist is a company's absolute front-line person. He or she is usually the first person a customer speaks to in person or on the phone. His or her duties typically include ...

✧ Greeting customers.

✧ Directing them to a specific person or department.

✧ Making or changing appointments.

✧ Answering customers' questions.

✧ Taking messages and informing other employees of a visitor's arrival.

✧ Performing basic duties such as bookkeeping and filing.

Although being a receptionist is an entry-level position, it holds a lot of power. As the front-line person, you'll serve as the gatekeeper, sometimes doing your boss the favor of not letting people in to see her or speak with her on the phone.

What it takes: You'll need a very friendly personality, along with the ability to say "no" to certain people (like when the bill collector comes by to get your boss to pay up and you need to explain that she simply isn't available right now). You need to have a good memory and be an accurate note-taker for all the messages people will leave. Keyboarding and switchboard skills are helpful and can also be learned on the job. In some businesses you may spend hours in a quiet office waiting for something to happen, in which case you'll have to be self-motivated in order to stay busy and avoid boredom. You'll also need to dress professionally and have a clear speaking voice.

Where the jobs are: Almost all organizations have receptionists, including medical offices, nonprofit organizations, government agencies, manufacturers, and service businesses. You'll find job postings for receptionists online and at government, nonprofit, and private employment agencies.

The Mosh Pit

Don't let shyness stop you from finding a receptionist job. Ask among your adult friends to see if they know of any openings where they work.

What this could lead to: After a successful job as a receptionist, you may decide to pursue a career in business administration, office management, word processing, or customer service.

The Hospitable Hotel Clerk

Front desk clerks are key to the operation of any lodging establishment. Here's what a front desk clerk does:

◇ Welcomes arriving guests

◇ Registers guests and gives them room keys

◇ Totals up the bill and takes payment at the end of the guest's stay

◇ Keeps records of room assignments and other information

◇ Answers guests' questions about hotel or community services

◇ Handles complaints or problems with the rooms

In a small establishment like a bed-and-breakfast, a front desk clerk may also handle phone reservations, deliver mail and messages to guests, perform simple bookkeeping, monitor the switchboard, and serve as concierge (the one who knows what's going on in town, how to get tickets, and all that stuff).

Although desk clerks don't make much in the way of tips, they do occasionally pocket some bills for their friendly service.

What it takes: Get your facial muscles in shape 'cause this job requires a lot of smiling, even with customers who aren't happy campers. A good pair of shoes and strong sense of organization will help you through your shift of standing at the reception desk. Familiarity with or eagerness to become familiar with office equipment and procedures is helpful since many details need to be recorded and kept straight.

Where the jobs are: Every hotel, motel, bed-and-breakfast, YMCA, and youth hostel needs someone to welcome guests. Look in the Yellow Pages to see what places are local to you.

Laser Pointer

Looking for a summer getaway? You could incorporate a summer away from home with making some decent money. Check out jobs in lodging establishments in a resort town you've always wanted to visit.

What this could lead to: Your experience as a hotel desk clerk may move you into a management position at the hotel. Or you may decide you like the hospitality biz so much you want to manage your own hotel, motel, or bed-and-breakfast someday.

Tell It to the Teller

A bank teller is the person standing behind the counter at a bank, doing any number of transactions with customers. In short, here's what a teller does:

✧ Cashes checks

✧ Receives deposits and loan payments

✧ Processes withdrawals

✧ Sells savings bonds and travelers' checks

✧ Counts and manages the cash in the cash drawer

In large banks, beginners start as limited-transaction tellers, performing clerical duties, cashing checks, and observing more complicated activities.

What it takes: I'm sure you guessed it: You've got to be good with numbers. If two plus two doesn't equal four for you, don't even think about this job. You need to be able to do simple math in your head, be willing to learn banking equipment such as 10-key punch machines, computers, calculators, faxes, copiers, coin-counting machines, and the good ol' lock and key for your cash drawer.

Customer service skills are also important. You must be professional in the way that you look and act, and you must be able to keep customers' financial matters confidential (no telling Aunt Snoopy that Owen Cash just took out a loan for 500 bucks).

Where the jobs are: You'll see banks and credit unions listed in your Yellow Pages, and you'll find them on college campuses and military bases.

What this could lead to: Your bank teller experience might lend itself to a career as a financial analyst, estate planner, stockbroker, accountant, bank manager, statistician, or math teacher.

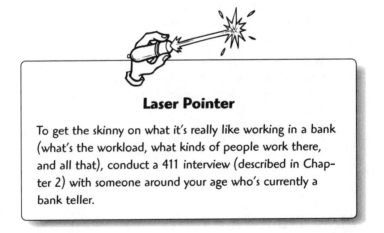

Laser Pointer

To get the skinny on what it's really like working in a bank (what's the workload, what kinds of people work there, and all that), conduct a 411 interview (described in Chapter 2) with someone around your age who's currently a bank teller.

Got Gas?

Gas station attendants work at the old-fashioned type of gas station where the driver says, "fill 'er up!" Because of the influx of self-serve stations and the rise in gas prices, these old-style stations aren't easy to find. But if you can get a job in one, here's what you'll be doing on the job:

✧ Greeting customers who drive up to the service pump

✧ Putting gas in their cars

✧ Checking the oil and possibly adding some

✧ Washing the front and rear windows

✧ Checking the air pressure of the tires

✧ Taking payments and making change

In many stations, the attendant acts as cashier for the station's convenience store and self-serve gas pumps. The attendant may spend time answering customers' questions, like "How do I get to Route 66 from here?"

What it takes: You need to be handy with simple mechanical tools such as the gas pump, the window squeegee, air pressure guage, and oil dispensers. Your knowledge of cars will be helpful, because you're bound to be asked a lot of basic questions, like "What kind of oil do you recommend for my car?" You'll need to learn how to use a cash register if you don't already know. And you'll need a full set of people skills to welcome drivers and help them out.

Where the jobs are: Look in the Yellow Pages to find gas stations and auto shops that offer full-service pumping. Or take a day in the sun and drive around to all the stations in your area.

What this could lead to: If you love working around cars, you may continue by becoming an auto mechanic, car salesperson, auto insurance agent, auto assembler, or rental car agent.

More Front-Line Jobs

Now that you have an idea of what front-line positions entail, can you think of other jobs like the ones listed so far in this chapter? Here are 10 more:

Customer service rep	Rental clerk
Door-to-door salesperson	Telemarketer

Manufacturer's sales rep

Ticket taker at movie theaters and events

Parking lot attendant

Tour guide

Pizza delivery guy (or gal)

Usher at concerts

Inside Dope

To get the buzz on jobs outside the United States, go to www.overseasjobs.com.

As you go through your day, notice what front-line workers you encounter. Would you like to do any of their jobs?

The Least You Need to Know

❖ A front-line position involves customer service, which requires an outgoing, friendly personality.

❖ Many front-line positions pay an hourly wage plus tips, bonuses, purchase discounts, or other perks.

❖ Restaurants and retail stores hire cashiers, hosts and hostesses, waiters and waitresses, food counter attendants, and salespeople—all front-line jobs.

❖ Offices, hotels, and banks employ front counter people to greet customers and initiate business.

❖ A few gas stations hire full-service gas attendants to give luxury attention to customers at the pump.

Supporting the Show

In This Chapter

✧ The role of a support person and why it might appeal to you

✧ Looking at administrative and customer service jobs

✧ Checking out possibilities in the delivery business

✧ Finding work that involves cleanup

In every movie there's a star and a supporting actor. A supporting actor's role is to make the star look great without drawing too much attention to him- or herself. In fact, the only time the supporting actor gets the spotlight is when the Oscars roll around.

In business there are supporting roles, too. These jobs may not be glamorous, but *nothing* would get done without them. And just as in the movies, people who work support jobs make the star (which in this case is the business) look totally awesome.

In this chapter you'll find details about support jobs that range from alphabetizing books in the library to squealing wheels as a bike messenger.

Supporting Actor

There are probably four reasons why you've turned to this chapter:

1. You circled 1a, 2a, 3a, 4a, or 4b on the "You've Got Personality" quiz in Chapter 2, "Your M.O. at Work."

2. The "What's Your Subject?" worksheet in Chapter 2 indicated that you'd be good at a support job.

3. You're making your way through all the job descriptions in Part 2, "Top Fifty Jobs," to see which ones grab you.

4. You want to learn which support jobs might help you get started in a particular career.

Those are all good reasons to check out the following essential behind-the-scenes positions:

Technical support person	Mail clerk
Administrative assistant	Messenger
Junior administrative assistant	Maid
Library assistant	Janitor
Dispatcher	Kitchen helper

Inside Dope

Average wages vary from state to state. To get the scoop on wages in your area, turn to Appendix A, "Agencies That Work," and contact your state's employment agency.

Entry-level jobs of this nature pay between minimum wage and a few dollars more than minimum wage, depending on the employee's skill level, the company, and in what part of the country the job is performed.

Read on to learn what's involved in doing each of these support jobs.

Tech Talk

Technical support employees help customers and users by giving them technical assistance and advice. They're troubleshooters who ...

⬧ Identify users' technical problems.

⬧ Answer their questions.

⬧ Walk them through their hardware, software, or systems difficulties.

⬧ Empathize with customers' frustrations.

⬧ Provide advice about other products sold by the company.

Tech support people may work by phone or in person, frequently using automated diagnostic programs.

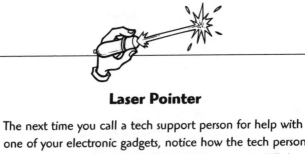

Laser Pointer

The next time you call a tech support person for help with one of your electronic gadgets, notice how the tech person conducts the conversation and what interpersonal skills he or she uses to fix your problem. Could you do that kind of work, and would you like it?

What it takes: To do this job, you should have a strong technical aptitude. Knowledge of and experience with computer systems will serve you well, along with a natural ability to pick up new technologies quickly (such as the *wigamajacker* the company sells). You should be a strong problem solver with analytical skills and a ton of patience because you could be helping beginning and exasperated customers jump through technical hoops. Good communication skills are important, too.

Where the jobs are: Large businesses sometimes need in-house technical support people to help their many employees use technical equipment such as computers, printers, modems, faxes, and copy machines. Tech supporters also work at manufacturers' help-desks, where they provide support to customers who have purchased a particular line of technical products. To find these jobs, check your Yellow Pages and go online to see what computer, software, or other technical product manufacturers are in your area.

What this could lead to: As a tech support person, you could discover that you want to pursue a career in electronic engineering, computer science, customer service, or business management.

Answering as an Administrative Assistant

An administrative assistant supports a manager in an office setting. An "admin," as this person is called, serves as the eyes, ears, and sometimes the voice, of the boss. This means ...

✧ Answering the phone.

✧ Making appointments.

✧ Keeping a calendar.

✧ Filing forms and other paperwork.

✧ Word-processing letters.

✧ Sending e-mails.

✧ Booking travel plans.

✧ Informing the boss when he or she has to be somewhere.

Luckily, there's a lot of gear (such as address databases, word processing software, online calendars, and spreadsheet applications) that makes the job easier. An admin might work solo for one manager or as part of a clerical team that supports a whole department.

Inside Dope

For in-depth analyses of administrative support positions, visit the Bureau of Labor Statistics Web page "Administrative Support Positions, Including Clerical" (stats.bls.gov/oco/oco1005.htm).

What it takes: Typing is a big one for an administrative assistant. You should be able to do anywhere from 50 to 90 words per minute—the faster the better, as long as you're accurate. Knowing a word processing program (MS Word for most offices) is important, as well as being good with spelling and grammar. You should be organized, able to file logically, and find things quickly.

Where the jobs are: Almost every office needs an admin. You might find an opening at a large corporation, small business, nonprofit organization, government agency, school, or hospital. You could also contact private employment agencies (found in the Yellow Pages) who frequently find administrative work for eager workers. Another great source of job postings is your employment development department. (See contact information for your state's employment agency in Appendix A.)

What this could lead to: As an administrative assistant you'll learn how an office or business runs in the real world.

Many admins advance to office managers, and some move on to training or supervisory positions in the company. Who knows, you may end up being the CEO of a corporation or even creating your own business someday!

Assistant to the Assistant

A junior administrative assistant is the assistant to the assistant. Some executive and administrative assistants have so many responsibilities that they need junior admins just to keep them rolling in copy machine toner and paper clips. A junior admin's job is to sweat the small but important stuff, like ...

- ✦ Running errands.
- ✦ Filing.
- ✦ Typing simple forms.
- ✦ Copying documents.
- ✦ Delivering messages.
- ✦ Putting paper in printers and copiers.
- ✦ Keeping office supplies handy, and ordering new supplies when they run low.

This position is ideal as a first-time job since it's a great way to see how businesses work without your having to handle too much responsibility.

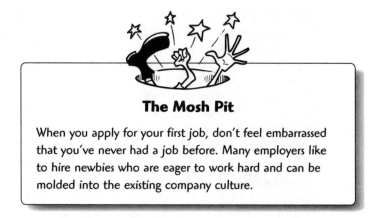

The Mosh Pit

When you apply for your first job, don't feel embarrassed that you've never had a job before. Many employers like to hire newbies who are eager to work hard and can be molded into the existing company culture.

What it takes: Because this is an entry-level job, you'll need to be able to follow instructions well and be eager to learn. For the most part you'll have supervision, which means you'll have someone to coach you through your day and answer questions as you go. With a willingness to do your job accurately and efficiently, you'll do great in this job. In no time, you'll realize that you're a valuable part of an administrative team that makes the company look great!

Where the jobs are: Look for junior administrative positions in large organizations such as government agencies, hospitals, corporations, and schools. You could also check with private employment agencies as well as your state employment agency for job postings (see Appendix A).

What this could lead to: This could be a stepping stone to positions like administrative assistant, office manager, and beyond, as outlined in the previous section.

Hanging Out in the Library Stacks

Library assistants, under the direction of librarians, help make libraries one of the most organized institutions around. These assistants keep the wheels greased by ...

✧ Updating patrons' records on computer databases.

✧ Stamping the due date on the material.

✧ Inspecting returned materials for damage.

✧ Sorting and shelving returned books and periodicals.

Because customers often need help navigating the library system, a library assistant sometimes serves as a guide in finding books, searching databases, and explaining how equipment is used.

What it takes: A love of reading is a big factor here, as well as an appreciation for organization, since a library is basically a big filing cabinet for books, magazines, and so on. Other valuable skills include patience, attention to detail, and sensitivity to all types of people including those with disabilities (such as the blind and hearing-impaired).

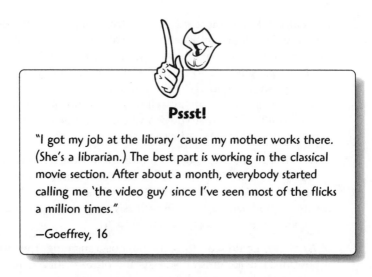

Pssst!

"I got my job at the library 'cause my mother works there. (She's a librarian.) The best part is working in the classical movie section. After about a month, everybody started calling me 'the video guy' since I've seen most of the flicks a million times."

—Goeffrey, 16

Where the jobs are: These jobs can be found at schools, and, naturally enough, your local public libraries.

What this could lead to: Library assistants can go on to become librarians or library technicians (the people who set up the databases and other technology). The skills learned in a library can also fit into other contexts, such as Web site development and corporate information technology (I.T.) management.

Calling All Cars

Dispatchers are the voices that keep delivery cars, trucks, and bicycles moving throughout the world. They're the ones who tell drivers where they should be and who (or what) to pick up. They usually work a specific shift (like 5 P.M. to midnight), and are expected to ...

- ✧ Answer calls from customers.
- ✧ Coordinate driving assignments.
- ✧ Give clear directions to drivers by radio.
- ✧ Keep records of calls they receive, orders they book, and jobs the drivers complete.

Make no mistake about it, dispatchers are the unseen people behind the smooth pickup and delivery of millions of people, packages, and services everyday.

What it takes: Communication skills. You hear me? I said c-o-m-m-u-n-i .... Seriously, you must be able to explain what you mean to people briefly and accurately. Be prepared to learn an entirely new lingo, full of shortcuts and abbreviations. You need to be comfortable on the phone, and be ready to deal with other communication technologies such as beepers, radios, cell phones, and e-mail.

Where the jobs are: You may not qualify to be on a 911 dispatch team until you're in your 20s (depending on the regulations in your state). However, managers in car towing, messenger, and trucking services should welcome your energy and enthusiasm.

What this could lead to: After a stint as a commercial dispatcher, you might want to become an emergency dispatcher, which in turn might lead to a career as a paramedic or ambulance driver. Or, who knows, maybe you'll get turned on by the sound of your voice and end up as a radio or TV announcer.

Laser Pointer

Good people skills are essential to all support jobs. You must be professional and friendly to your boss, co-workers, and the company's clients. And you'll need to be able to take direction from your manager and those around you who are more experienced.

Takin' It to the Street

Mail clerks handle letters and packages in large organizations such as businesses, nonprofits, and the government. (Nope, I'm not talking about the people you see with "U.S. Postal Service" on their caps.) Mail clerks perform a number of important duties behind the scenes, such as ...

◇ Sorting incoming mail.

◇ Delivering mail within the organization.

◇ Preparing outgoing mail.

◇ Coordinating pickups with courier services like FedEx and UPS.

◇ Tracking incoming and outgoing mail with computers.

◇ Collating, folding, and stuffing packets for bulk mailings.

In many businesses, these tasks require using scales and machines for stamping, collating, folding, and copying.

What it takes: To be a mail clerk you must be careful and dependable. You must be able to do routine tasks and work well with your hands. Also, be ready to learn all the various classes of postage (first, third, bulk, and so on). Finally, some mail clerks need drivers' licenses in order to deliver mail among several buildings.

What this could lead to: Depending on the size of the operation, mail clerks can advance to supervisors and office managers. Others transfer to related jobs within the U.S. Postal Service.

Where the jobs are: Look for mail clerk jobs in government agencies, colleges and universities, hospitals, banks, legal services, businesses, and large nonprofit organizations.

Instant Messenger

A messenger does what Instant Messenger does on the Internet: He or she moves stuff from here to there. Instant

Messenger moves data from one computer to another, whereas a living, breathing messenger delivers things from one place to another. Those things could be contracts, small packages, portfolios, or, who knows, pianos. (Well, okay, maybe not pianos.)

Inside Dope

For more details about service positions, go to the Bureau of Labor Statistics Web page "Service Occupations" (stats.bls.gov/oco/oco1006.htm).

Messengers (also called couriers) work mostly during regular business hours (9 A.M. to 5 P.M.). Their responsibilities run like this:

✧ Getting an assignment from a dispatcher

✧ Picking up the material from the sender

✧ Delivering the package to its destination

✧ Reporting to the dispatcher that the package was delivered

✧ Keeping accurate records of pickups and deliveries

In most cases where a messenger is used, a company needs a valuable package delivered securely by a certain time. And they pay good money for someone to do that by foot, bike, or car.

What it takes: A messenger who works for a company that services five square miles or more may need a valid driver's license, a registered and inspected vehicle, a good driving record, and insurance coverage. Some messengers are even required to provide and maintain their own vehicles.

If you're in a city, you might be able to get a job as a bike messenger. Some people love this kind of work, which keeps them outdoors most of the time. As a bike messenger, your first priority must be safety, especially on city streets where traffic is heavy.

Whether you deliver by car, bike, or on foot, knowledge of the area, the ability to read maps, and a good sense of direction are important.

Where the jobs are: Here are some places where you'll find messengers employed: government agencies, colleges and universities, newspaper agencies, hospitals, medical and dental laboratories, banks, legal services, and, of course, courier services.

The Mosh Pit

Be realistic about how well your qualifications match a position's requirements. For instance, if a job requires you to have a driver's license and you don't have one, don't go for the job. And never lie to the employer just to get the job. Lies can hurt your job recommendations.

What this could lead to: Being a messenger could lead to an interest in other outdoor work, such as mail carrier or route driver. Most likely, your stint as a messenger will introduce you to the world of business, where you might take an administrative position or even start your own courier service.

Got It Maid

Maids do cleaning work, typically in hotels, motels, or bed and breakfasts. Although maids seldom interact directly with customers, they play a key role in making guests feel welcome by making rooms and lobby areas clean and comfortable. A maid's duties usually include ...

✧ Vacuuming carpets.

✧ Mopping floors.

✧ Dusting.

✧ Cleaning bathrooms.

✧ Washing the inside of windows and mirrors.

✧ Making beds.

✧ Replacing soiled towels with clean ones.

As a maid, you're apt to get tips, so keep your eyes peeled for bills that might be left under pillows or on counter tops in the rooms you clean.

What it takes: Employers usually look for dependable, hardworking people who are in good health, follow directions well, and get along with other people. The ideal candidate is someone who gets fulfillment from seeing the dramatic before-and-after effect of her work.

Where the jobs are: Look for these jobs in hotels, motels, bed and breakfasts, apartment complexes, and large vacation resorts. There are also cleaning services that hire maids to work for them. Check your Yellow Pages under "Maids."

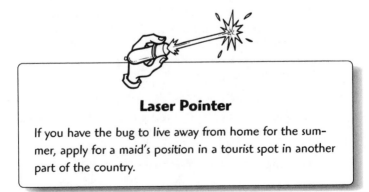

Laser Pointer

If you have the bug to live away from home for the summer, apply for a maid's position in a tourist spot in another part of the country.

What this could lead to: As a maid, you might become interested in pursuing a career in hotel management, or you might discover an interest in the chemical products industry. Another possibility is to open your own cleaning service someday with a team of maids who work in people's homes.

Cleaning Up as a Janitor

Janitors perform a wide range of tasks and they're found in almost every kind of business setting: office buildings, apartment buildings, hospitals, schools, and stores. On the job, janitors do the following:

- ❖ Wet- and dry-mop floors
- ❖ Polish smooth floors
- ❖ Vacuum carpets
- ❖ Clean bathrooms
- ❖ Keep supplies available in bathrooms
- ❖ Make repairs
- ❖ Empty trashcans
- ❖ Paint
- ❖ Sweep walkways and possibly shovel snow

This job is perfect for someone who always said "glad to" when Mom asked him to do chores.

What it takes: Dependable, hard-working people are most likely to find work in this field. You must be a "can do" person, and be comfortable working both under direction and alone, in some cases in the middle of the night when the business is closed.

Where the jobs are: Janitors usually find work by answering newspaper ads, applying directly to organizations (mentioned earlier) where they would like to work, contacting property management firms, joining local labor unions, or visiting state employment agencies where job openings are posted.

What this could lead to: A janitor might move into a career in inventory management, construction, gardening, pest control, or property management. As an entrepreneur, he may get into repair work or the hauling business.

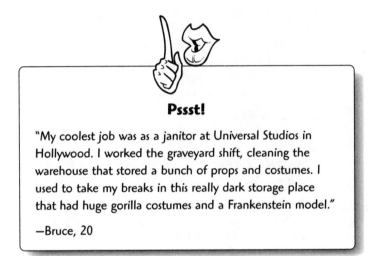

Pssst!

"My coolest job was as a janitor at Universal Studios in Hollywood. I worked the graveyard shift, cleaning the warehouse that stored a bunch of props and costumes. I used to take my breaks in this really dark storage place that had huge gorilla costumes and a Frankenstein model."

—Bruce, 20

Slice 'n' Dice

Kitchen workers are the behind-the-scenes people who keep a restaurant running. In some restaurants, they ...

✧ Slice or chop vegetables.

✧ Measure ingredients.

✧ Stir simmering soups.

✧ Cut and clean meat and seafood.

✧ Wash pots and pans.

✧ Run dishwashers.

✧ Clean work areas and cutting boards.

✧ Organize storage areas such as walk-in refrigerators, freezers, and cabinets.

✧ Run errands.

This is a great job for those who love food—and who doesn't? As a kitchen helper, you're bound to be trying out lots of tasty dishes while filling an essential niche on the cooking team.

What it takes: This job takes a good disposition and a willingness to learn and work hard. Kitchens can sometimes be like pressure cookers—they're hot and work needs to be done quickly. There's room for questions but not for complaining in this fast-paced workplace. You may also need some strong muscles for carrying large boxes, pots, and pans.

Where the jobs are: Look anywhere food is prepared and served, such as restaurants, cafeterias, coffee shops, diners, and cafés. Kitchen help positions are often advertised in the newspaper or on signs that hang in the establishment's front window.

What this could lead to: As a kitchen worker you could advance to an assistant or short-order cook, and could eventually become a restaurant manager, head chef, recipe developer, recipe book writer, or food critic.

More Behind-the-Scenes Jobs

There are countless other support jobs available. Here are 10 more that you could consider:

Busperson	Laundry and dry cleaning machine operator
Cannery worker	Proofreader
Copy editor	Stagehand
Factory assembler	Vending machine workers
Grocery stocker and bagger	Web site content consultant

Inside Dope

Peterson's Summer Jobs for Students (published annually by Peterson's Thomson Learning) details more than 55,000 positions, including employers' names and contact info throughout North America.

You can probably think of even more support work, and you'll certainly run into some jobs that will fit your job M.O. (discussed in Chapter 2).

The Least You Need to Know

✦ Taking a support job is a great way to learn about a business without having to handle too much responsibility.

✦ As a support employee, you'll do many behind-the-scenes tasks that will play an important part in making operations run smoothly.

✦ Administrative work requires you to work in an office environment using computers, faxes, copiers, and other equipment.

✦ Delivery jobs are links in the systems that move people, information, and products around the world.

✦ Support service workers keep business areas clean, safe, and healthy.

Doin' It with Heart

In This Chapter

✧ Work that comes from the heart and helps others

✧ Care-giving jobs that make a difference for children and people who are sick

✧ Fun-loving jobs that show kids of all ages how to have a good time

✧ Working with animals to keep them healthy and beautiful

If you love helping people, animals, or both, you're a big-hearted person. Having a big heart is a good thing, 'cause everyone loves being with someone who's kind, considerate, and giving.

In this chapter you'll find 10 ways to put your big heart to work, and don't be surprised to find that some of them involve having a lot of fun, too.

Places of the Heart

There are a few reasons why you might have turned to this chapter. My guess is that at least one of the following is true:

1. You selected 1a, 1b, 2a, 3b, 4b, or 5b for one or more of your answers on the "You've Got Personality" quiz in Chapter 2, "Your M.O. at Work."

2. Either social studies, science, music and the arts, or gym is your favorite subject in school. (See the "What's Your Subject?" worksheet in Chapter 2.)

3. You're reading all the job descriptions in Part 2, "Top Fifty Jobs," to see if one catches your eye.

4. You know you want a job that values your big heart and wonder what careers it might lead to.

Whatever the reason, you're here and you're about to learn the ins and outs of 10 jobs that involve helping people or animals. Here are the job descriptions you'll find:

Baby-sitter or nanny	Swimming instructor
Daycare assistant	Amusement park attendant
Home companion	Zookeeper's helper
Nurse's aide	Kennel attendant
Camp counselor	Dog and cat groomer

The actual amount of pay for these jobs, of course, depends on the organization you work for, what part of the country you work in, and exactly what level of responsibility you carry.

Okay, you big-hearted person, read on to learn about 10 caring jobs.

The Mosh Pit

If money's your biggest motivator for getting a job, stay away from the ones described in this chapter. These jobs don't pay a lot (minimum wage or a little more); the rewards come in the feel-good department. The satisfaction of helping a sick person or teaching a child a new skill is something money can't come close to. (However, many of these jobs can lead to higher paying careers.)

Just Call Me Nanny

Baby-sitters and nannies work in a home setting taking care of children from birth to age 10 or older. They're responsible for ...

✧ Bathing, dressing, and feeding children.

✧ Changing diapers and washing clothes.

✧ Supervising play.

✧ Reading to the kids.

✧ Putting them to bed and waking them up.

✧ Cleaning the children's rooms and play areas.

Baby-sitters work for an hourly wage and may be hired for just a few hours (for instance, when parents go out for an evening) or a full eight-hour day (for example, when the parents are at work). A nanny typically lives with the family and gets paid by the week or month.

Laser Pointer

As a nanny, you'd get your room, meals, and paycheck, as well as possible perks like vacations with the family that you're employed by. (How does a trip to Bali sound to you?)

What it takes: You must love children in order to be a good baby-sitter or nanny. That means being creative, patient, and caring. An awareness of child safety issues is important, as well as knowing first aid. Some states issue child care certificates for those who take a course in CPR (cardiopulmonary resuscitation) for children.

You should be a decent cook (or at least be able to use a microwave), be neat, courteous, and trustworthy. You'll also need to have physical stamina.

Where the jobs are: Look in the classified section of your newspaper and local bulletin boards to find notices of families that need help with kids in their homes. You could also check your Yellow Pages to find a child-care employment agency.

What this could lead to: Many baby-sitters and nannies become teachers. Others become child-care development specialists, psychologists, and authors of children's books.

Kidding Around

Daycare assistants (also called child-care assistants or preschool teacher's assistants) nurture and teach preschool children, ages two through five, in group settings. Their work is a lot of fun and games with the clear purpose of helping children prepare for their first year of school, as well as building strong foundations for social, intellectual, and physical development. Here's what a child-care assistant generally does:

- ✧ Greets children when they arrive and helps them remove their coats
- ✧ Engages them in activities that develop their interests and talents
- ✧ Creates opportunities for developing social skills with other children
- ✧ Provides quiet time for rest
- ✧ Feeds children, teaching them good eating habits and personal hygiene
- ✧ Identifies children who don't feel well or show signs of developmental problems

As a child-care assistant, you'll be on a team with certified preschool teachers. As a team member, you may meet with parents individually and in groups to discuss a child's program, progress, or challenges.

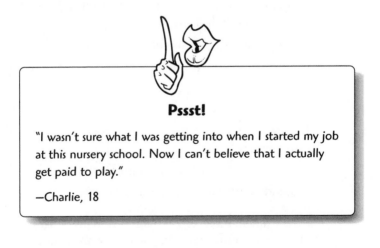

Pssst!

"I wasn't sure what I was getting into when I started my job at this nursery school. Now I can't believe that I actually get paid to play."

—Charlie, 18

What it takes: To be a good child-care assistant, you must be alert, enthusiastic, and creative. You must anticipate and prevent problems, deal with disruptive children, and be able to give fair discipline. Clear communication to children and their parents is important, as well as to other teachers on the team. Skills in music, art, drama, and storytelling are highly valued.

Where the jobs are: Preschool facilities (also called daycare centers or nursery schools) can be found in private homes, schools, religious organizations, and corporations that provide child care for their employees. Look in the Yellow Pages under "Child Care," read local newspapers, and ask parents with small children where they send their kids.

What this could lead to: In addition to the career paths mentioned for baby-sitters and nannies, a child-care worker may become a preschool director or run a daycare center out of the home.

Home Alone ... *Not!*

Home companions (also known as personal attendants) are highly valued caregivers to elderly, handicapped, or convalescent people. Aside from being good company to his or her patient, a caregiver does the following:

- ✧ Helps with bathing and dressing
- ✧ Prepares and serves meals
- ✧ Goes shopping
- ✧ Keeps the house tidy
- ✧ Plays cards and board games, and goes on walks with the patient
- ✧ Takes them to medical appointments
- ✧ Handles social and business affairs

Above all, a home companion is a friend to his or her patient. Depending upon the situation, you may be the person's primary caregiver or you may work on a team composed of family, friends, and professionals.

Pssst!

"I take care of a 92-year-old woman in her home two hours a day on the weekends. But I think about her a lot and sometimes check in on her and take her little presents during the week even though it's not part of my job. It makes me feel good."

—Debbie, 16

What it takes: This job requires compassion, empathy, and patience. You will also need knowledge of basic first aid and be safety conscious at all times. Physical strength is necessary since you're apt to be doing a lot of lifting and carrying. A talent for organization will also come in handy.

Where the jobs are: Word of mouth is one of the best ways to find this kind of work. Ask friends and adults if they know of a homebound person who could use some help. Also inquire at senior centers, nursing homes, convalescent centers, and organizations for the chronically ill (such as the Multiple Sclerosis Society) to see where you can fill a home-care need. Help Wanted ads in the newspaper are another good place to find these jobs.

What this could lead to: After serving as a home-care companion, you may feel called to a career in healthcare as a nurse, doctor, nutritionist, occupational therapist, physical therapist, or hospital administrator.

Coming to a Nurse's Aid

Nurse's aides perform a significant role in hospitals and nursing facilities. They not only help nurses, they also offer cheer and warmth to patients, many of whom are in pain, afraid, or just plain bored. In addition to being friendly faces, nurse's aides ...

✧ Answer patients' call bells.

✧ Deliver messages.

✧ Serve meals.

✧ Make beds.

✧ Help patients eat, dress, and bathe.

✧ Provide skin care.

✧ Take temperature, pulse, respiration, and blood pressure.

Nurse's aides are members of the caregiving team along with nurses, doctors, and physical therapists. In nursing homes, the nurse's aide sometimes is the primary caregiver for a number of long-term patients and develops meaningful relationships with them.

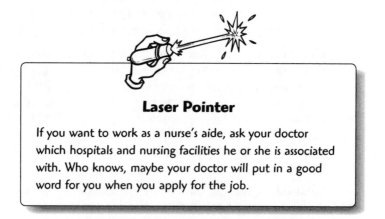

Laser Pointer

If you want to work as a nurse's aide, ask your doctor which hospitals and nursing facilities he or she is associated with. Who knows, maybe your doctor will put in a good word for you when you apply for the job.

What it takes: To do well as a nurse's aide, you must have a strong desire to help people. You should be able to work as part of a team, have good communication skills, and be willing to do repetitive tasks. Patience, understanding, emotional stability, dependability, and good listening skills are all highly valued in this job.

Where the jobs are: Nurse's aides are employed in hospitals, nursing homes, and personal care facilities. A quick look in the Yellow Pages will tell you the facilities in your area.

What this could lead to: This is an excellent way to see if you'd like a career in the medical field. If all goes well, you might become a nurse, doctor, physical therapist, medical technician, or pharmacist.

Pitching to Be a Camp Counselor

Camp counselors work at overnight and day camps for children. As an entry-level counselor you would help more experienced counselors with the following responsibilities:

◇ Giving instruction in activities such as swimming, horseback riding, archery, boating, music, drama, gymnastics, tennis, and computers

◇ Guiding campers in their daily living and general socialization development

◇ Supervising entertainment such as campfire sing-alongs, cookouts, hikes, and contests

◇ Comforting kids who are homesick and resolve conflicts that might arise among campers

If you're thinking about being a camp counselor, you've probably been to camp yourself and have a sense of what's involved in the job. Your understanding of the difficulties young campers go through will help you be a good coach to them.

What this takes: Camp counselors must be outgoing and good at motivating others (you've got to be able to rally the troops early in the morning to do such things as jump into an icy lake). At the same time, you need to be sensitive to campers' needs, challenges, and fears, and be able to adapt activities to meet those needs. Other qualities that make a counselor good: creativity, resourcefulness, and leadership. You must be able to perform first aid and handle unexpected crises.

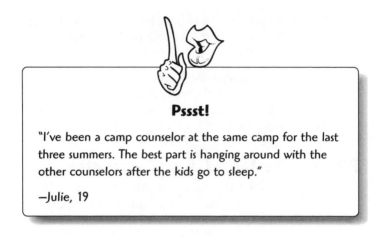

Pssst!

"I've been a camp counselor at the same camp for the last three summers. The best part is hanging around with the other counselors after the kids go to sleep."

—Julie, 19

Where the jobs are: Overnight and day camps are sponsored by nonprofit groups (like the Girl Scouts of America), religious groups (like Jewish Community Centers), and civic associations (like your local community recreational center). Go to each of these in your area and ask the recreation director what camp counselor positions are open.

What this could lead to: Camp counselors often make excellent teachers, civic leaders, sports coaches, recreational directors, guidance counselors, social workers, and psychotherapists.

Counting Laps

A swimming instructor can be a child's favorite teacher. While teaching a kid a valuable skill, a swimming instructor gives a child a wonderful way to play safely and have fun with other kids. Here's what a swimming instructor does:

✧ Determines the level of the child's ability and designs lessons for him or her

✧ Instructs the child in how to dive and do specific swimming strokes

✧ Corrects the child's technique and motivates him or her to practice

✧ Teaches safe water play and organizes team water sports

✧ Takes care of equipment such as floats, life jackets, balls, first-aid kits, and life-saving gear

If you love the water, enjoy hearing children scream with delight, and like to help kids learn new things, this could be the job for you.

Inside Dope

Read the article "Summer Jobs That Get You in Shape" (at www.efit.com/servlet/article/teens/18136.html) to learn about outdoor jobs you might be interested in.

What this takes: A swimming instructor must pass certain courses and be certified in areas such as first aid, CPR, and life saving. In some states, age requirements may exist. You must be patient, speak clearly, be organized, and love children. Your ability to understand and motivate is key because many kids are afraid of the water and need help overcoming their fears.

Where the jobs are: Look for swim instructor positions at any of the day and overnight camps mentioned earlier. A camp that has either a swimming pool or access to the waterfront of a lake or ocean will probably offer swimming lessons to its campers.

What this could lead to: Once you've been a swimming instructor you may go on to become a professional athlete (do the Olympic Games have any appeal to you?), gym teacher, sports coach, sports broadcaster, sports columnist, camp director, or social worker.

High on Rides

Amusement park attendants are the guys and gals at the
theme parks who make it all happen. Depending upon
exactly what position you hold, you could find yourself
doing the following:

✧ Setting up games

✧ Taking tickets

✧ Securing people in their seats before amusement park
rides take off

✧ Operating ride machines

✧ Performing as a clown or other character

✧ Cleaning up game and ride areas

✧ Managing crowds and lines of people

It sounds like a big game, but there's a lot of work involved
in this job. Side benefits include free or reduced entrance fees
for yourself, friends, and family.

What it takes: Lots of stamina and the ability to do repetitious tasks with a smile. You must be comfortable in crowds,
noise, and laughter (now that doesn't sound too hard). In
some positions, you may need to be physically strong (for
instance, if you have to lift dumbbells into place for the
record-holding weightlifter). Amusement parks usually prefer
workers who are at least 17 years old.

Where the jobs are: If you're an amusement park junkie, you
already know where the parks are. If not, look in the Yellow
Pages to find theme parks, amusement parks, go-cart rental
places, rodeos, miniature-golf courses, waterslide parks, and
skating rinks. Check the newspaper for upcoming small-town
carnivals and county fairs that need temporary help, usually
in the summer or early fall.

What this could lead to: Watch out, this job could lead to
lots of fun as an amusement park manager, camp director,
city recreation worker, P.E. teacher, hotel manager, or any career that involves customer service.

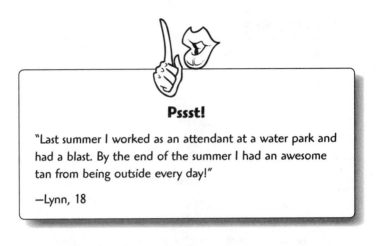

Pssst!

"Last summer I worked as an attendant at a water park and had a blast. By the end of the summer I had an awesome tan from being outside every day!"

—Lynn, 18

Keeping Up at the Zoo

Zookeeper's helpers assist zookeepers to take care of animals, many whose names I can't even pronounce. Here's what a zookeeper and his helper's day looks like:

- ✧ Prepares food to meet special animal diets
- ✧ Cleans enclosures where the animals live
- ✧ Assists in raising very young ones
- ✧ Watches for signs of illness, injury, eating disorders, and behavior changes
- ✧ Answers questions and ensures that the visiting public respects the zoo's rules

As a zookeeper's helper, you might find yourself caring for a broad group of animals (like mammals, birds, or reptiles), or you may work with a small collection of animals such as primates, large cats, or small mammals.

What it takes: You've got to love animals and be able to follow directions to a T. As a beginning zookeeper's helper, you'll need to be physically strong, a quick learner, and extremely safety conscious.

Where the jobs are: Hmmm, let's see ... in zoos? Similar jobs may be found in animal safari theme parks, circuses, and nature preserve exhibits.

The Mosh Pit

No matter how much you love animals, if you're allergic to their fur or dander, don't go near any of these animal care-giving jobs. Instead, find a position with an animal advocacy group, a publication about animals, or somewhere that doesn't deal directly with the furry critters.

Kennel Care

Kennel attendants take care of small companion animals like cats and dogs in boarding facilities while their owners are out of town. A beginning attendant does basic tasks like ...

✧ Cleaning cages and dog runs.

✧ Filling food and water dishes.

✧ Exercising the animals through walks and play.

✧ Bathing animals.

✧ Trimming nails and doing other grooming duties

Aside from working with the animals, an attendant may spend time in the reception area accepting new pets into the kennel, selling food and supplies, and helping with obedience training.

What it takes: If you're the kind of person who can't get enough of cats and dogs, this job is the one for you—you'll get your heart's desire in every size, shape, and color.

Kindness to animals is essential, along with an understanding of a dog or cat's need for companionship and its distress when separated from its owner. You must be able to interact well with people too, since they're the real customers in the kennel business. Your ability to follow directions will be helpful, because you'll need to abide by specific dietary instructions for the good of the animal.

Where the jobs are: You can find a job as a kennel assistant in dog and cat kennels, as well as through the Humane Society of the United States, the American Humane Association, the National Animal Control Association, and your city's animal control agency (otherwise known as "da pound"). Your local humane society is a good place to start (check the Yellow Pages).

What this could lead to: You could become a veterinarian, animal surgeon, or one of the less traditional animal professionals who specialize in chiropractic, acupuncture, and massage. You might also become a professional dog walker or kennel manager.

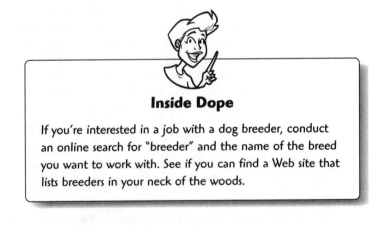

Inside Dope

If you're interested in a job with a dog breeder, conduct an online search for "breeder" and the name of the breed you want to work with. See if you can find a Web site that lists breeders in your neck of the woods.

Waggers and Groomers

Dog and cat groomers' helpers are a special breed. They specialize in making little critters look beautiful, much the way a hair stylist fashions a lady's hairdo. Grooming a pet involves these steps:

✧ Doing an initial brush-out of the fur

✧ Clipping the fur using electric clippers, combs, and grooming shears

✧ Trimming the nails

✧ Cleaning the ears

✧ Bathing and blow-drying the animal

✧ Performing the final clipping and styling

Groomers' helpers also deal with pet owners. They answer the phone, schedule appointments, discuss special aesthetic and veterinary needs, and report any medical problems (like skin or ear infections) they notice during the grooming.

What it takes: Pet groomers's helpers need to be able to read an animal's body (and vocal) language and feel comfortable working closely with different animal dispositions. Safety is always a high priority to avoid getting bitten or scratched. Knowledge of animal health is extremely helpful, although you'll certainly learn it on the job. You'll also need to have good people skills to speak with customers, poise to deal with emergencies (like dog fights in the back room), and a deep love for animals. Your artistic side will also be appreciated by the employer, customers, and, who knows, maybe even the beautifully coifed pets.

Where the jobs are: The most obvious places to apply for grooming positions are pet grooming shops (listed in the good ol' Yellow Pages). Also inquire at dog kennels, animal shelters, veterinary clinics, and pet supply stores.

What this could lead to: As a result of your job as a pet groomers' helper, you might pursue one of the careers mentioned for kennel attendant. However, you might also use your artistic talent to become a hair stylist, animal photographer, or theatrical pet trainer.

More Jobs for the Big-Hearted

There are, of course, lots more jobs that appeal to big-hearted people. Here are 10 more:

After-school program assistant	Personal shopper
Dog walker	Psychiatric nurse's aide
Horse groomer	Ski lift attendant
Lifeguard	Veterinarian's assistant
Livestock animal handler	Wildlife preserve worker

Laser Pointer

If none of the jobs mentioned in this chapter seem to fit your care-giving talents, consider working in a plant nursery. Plants need TLC, too!

Now that you're aware of jobs that help people or animals, you're bound to notice them all around you. Maybe one of those mentioned here will ring true for your big heart.

The Least You Need to Know

◇ Care-giving jobs don't usually pay high wages but they are very rewarding for the right type of person.

◇ Jobs that work with children include baby-sitters, pre-school teacher's assistants, camp counselors, and swimming instructors.

◇ Home companions and nurse's aides help elderly, disabled, and convalescent patients.

◇ Amusement park attendants work at making sure others have fun.

◇ If you love animals, consider a job as a zookeeper's helper, kennel attendant, or pet groomer.

Chapter 6

Sweatin' It Out

In This Chapter

✧ Who's cut out for manual labor

✧ Outside work that makes a difference

✧ Carrying on in the warehouse or recycling yard

✧ Making cars shine for money

✧ Picking and packaging fruits and veggies

"Hard work" isn't just a pair of four-letter words. For a lot of us, physical work is one of the most satisfying experiences there is. Coming home from a day of lifting, carrying, pounding, and digging feels better than the rush Bill Gates gets from counting his billions (well, okay, maybe Bill's got one up on us).

If you're one of those manual-labor lovers, this chapter is for you. We're going to cover jobs that make you sweat, and, as Martha Stewart says, that's a good thing.

A Job That Works

Finding a good job isn't hard, especially when you know what type of work you want. This chapter about manual labor grabbed your attention for one of the following reasons:

1. In the "You've Got Personality" quiz in Chapter 2, "Your M.O. at Work," you chose 1a, 3a, and/or 4b.

2. When it comes to your favorite school subject, you picked science, gym, or tech.

3. In an effort to be thorough, you're reading all the job descriptions in Part 2, "Top Fifty Jobs."

4. In order to start a career that involves doing or managing manual labor, you need to find a job that gets you headed in that direction.

That being the case, you're ready to read about the following 10 jobs described in this chapter:

Landscape worker	Recyclable material collector
Groundskeeper	Carwasher
Construction helper	Bellhop
Deckhand on a fishing boat	Farm worker
Warehouse person	Mover

The Mosh Pit

Don't despair about entry-level wages. In some cases you may be able to join a trade union for your job in manual labor, in which case you'll be working for union wages. That could be way cool!

As an entry-level manual laborer, you'll get paid minimum wage or a little more, depending upon the industry you work in, who's paying you, and what part of the country you're in.

Yard Control

Landscape workers do a variety of things, depending on what type of landscape project they're working on. This work is labor-intensive and incredibly rewarding for those who love plants. Here's what a landscape worker does:

- ✧ Plants and transplants vegetation
- ✧ Mulches gardens
- ✧ Fertilizes the soil
- ✧ Waters plants
- ✧ Prunes plants, trees, and shrubs
- ✧ Mows and waters lawns

Landscape workers may work alone or on teams, caring for either residential or commercial properties.

What it takes: A successful landscape worker loves getting his or her hands in the dirt, nurturing plants, and doing the heavy labor of digging and carrying bags of soil, seeds, and so forth. You must be able to follow directions well since plant care is an exact science. Teamwork is important for some jobs, as well as those good communications skills you've learned in school.

Where the jobs are: Apply for landscape jobs at, strangely enough, landscaping companies, as well as real estate and property management agencies (listed in the phone book).

What this could lead to: Those who fall in love with landscaping often pursue careers in botany, park management, landscape architecture, farming, forest conservation, and environmental science. Some open their own plant nurseries or landscaping businesses.

Laser Pointer

The next time you see a truck with lawn mowers and leaf blowers sticking out of it, take note of the company name painted on the side of the cab. A quick call to them might land you a landscape job.

Cuttin' Up in the Grass

Groundskeepers (also referred to as ground maintenance personnel) work for facilities such as athletic fields, golf courses, and parks. They do many of the things a landscape worker does, as well as ...

✧ Rake and mulch leaves.

✧ Clear snow from sidewalks and parking lots.

✧ Apply pesticides.

✧ Adjust plant irrigation systems to water plants and conserve water.

✧ Maintain and repair pools, fences, planters, benches, and cement surfaces.

A big difference between a groundskeeper and a landscaper is that the former works in the same place every day (a particular golf course, for instance) and the latter travels from property to property. As a beginning groundskeeper, you would assist an experienced worker in doing these chores, taking on more responsibility as you grew in the job.

The Mosh Pit

If you're worried about not having enough excitement in your job as a groundskeeper, look for work at a professional athletic field where you'll play the important role of maintaining the turf for your winning team.

What it takes: Attention to details and the big picture will take you far in this job. You'll need to follow instructions carefully with hand and power equipment, work well with your groundskeeping crew, and enjoy sweating in the sun. (By the way, don't forget your sunscreen.)

Where the jobs are: Your best bet is to check out institutions in your area such as schools, colleges, state and local parks and recreation departments, golf courses, hotels, cemeteries, and athletic fields. On a sunny afternoon, drive around your neighborhood to spot large amounts of manicured green, where a groundskeeper might be needed.

What this could lead to: This job could head you in many of the directions mentioned earlier for the landscape worker. Other career choices include athletic turf manager, golf course developer, and hardware store manager (or owner).

Construction Worker on Site

Construction helpers are the ones who run around assisting skilled construction workers. In short, they ...

✧ Carry tools, materials, and equipment for various construction workers such as electricians, carpenters, and plumbers.

✧ Run errands.

✧ Perform tasks using hand tools such as hammers, saws, wrenches, and pliers.

✧ Clean work areas at the end of each day.

Work as a construction helper can be a real eye-opener. How else could you get an insider's look at the construction of buildings, bridges, roads, or monuments?

What it takes: As a construction helper, you'll need to have dexterity to use the tools, excellent judgment when it comes to safety, and a high level of precision when making measurements. Following directions is key, along with physical strength and stamina. Interpersonal qualities such as honesty, dependability, and courtesy will do you well. Good math skills will also come in handy.

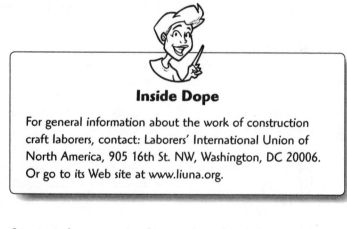

Inside Dope

For general information about the work of construction craft laborers, contact: Laborers' International Union of North America, 905 16th St. NW, Washington, DC 20006. Or go to its Web site at www.liuna.org.

Some employers require that you be at least 18, pass drug tests, and agree to background checks.

Where the jobs are: Look in the Yellow Pages under "Construction," "Carpentry," "Plumbing," "Electrical," and other construction-related topics for the names of potential employers. Also, look in the newspaper for Help Wanted ads and check with your area's labor unions to see if there's work.

What this could lead to: From your experience as a construction helper, you might decide to become an apprentice to a specific trade (such as plumbing or carpentry), which could lead you to the next level of journeyperson, and then on to master plumber, carpenter, or whatever your field. From there you could become a foreperson for a construction company, become a general contractor, or start your own construction company.

Getting Hooked on Fishing

Deckhands on fishing boats are entry-level positions that involve a lot of hard work and lots of learning. If you've always loved goin' fishing with your dad or uncle, here's a chance to do it for real. Grab your rubber boots and get on board with a commercial fishing outfit, where you'll ...

- ✦ Load equipment and supplies.
- ✦ Untie lines from other boats and docks.
- ✦ Use dip nets to keep small fish from escaping from the big nets.
- ✦ Wash, salt, ice, and stow away fish.
- ✦ Clean decks.
- ✦ Secure the boat lines and unload fish onto the dock.

Smaller fishing operations may allow beginners to handle more responsibility, such as hauling traps, operating fishing gear, and extracting the catch.

What it takes: This job requires a lot of physical strength and a hunger for adventure, because weather and water conditions can change quickly and become dangerous. Teamwork is critical to ensuring safety and success for a fishing venture. Other desirable qualities include mechanical aptitude, good coordination, endurance, patience, and alertness. And of course, you need a strong stomach (if you're prone to seasickness, this isn't the job for you).

Where the jobs are: Fishing vessels are owned by individuals, commercial fishing companies, marine biology labs, and sport fishing companies.

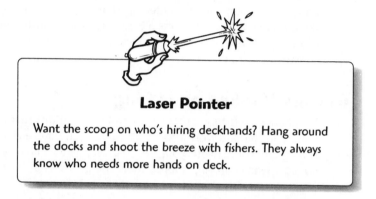

Laser Pointer

Want the scoop on who's hiring deckhands? Hang around the docks and shoot the breeze with fishers. They always know who needs more hands on deck.

What this could lead to: You might end up as captain of a fishing boat, owner of a fishing company, or manager of a retail fishing equipment store. Or you might become a merchant marine officer, harbor pilot, game warden, fishing guide, wildlife specialist, or marine biologist.

Where's the Warehouse Person?

Warehouse workers are essential to the storage and shipping of a company's merchandise. A warehouse person typically does the following:

✧ Moves materials from loading docks to storage areas

✧ Records incoming and outgoing shipments

✧ Organizes storage areas

✧ Keeps inventory records up to date

✧ Delivers items from the warehouse to the shipping area or loading dock

If this job seems like brainless work, think again. Boxes and packages have to be organized, counted, and moved carefully.

In industries dealing with perishable or fragile products, thousands of dollars worth of merchandise is entrusted to the warehouse person's care. That's no joke!

What it takes: Good math skills and a strong sense of organization will take you far in this field. You'll be on your feet most of the time and carrying heavy items, so physical strength and stamina are important. Your excellent interpersonal skills will also pay off since you'll be coordinating lots of details with customers, managers, and fellow workers.

Where the jobs are: Businesses that have warehouses include manufacturers, distributors, shipping services (like UPS and FedEx), couriers, and airlines. Grocery stores and department stores sometimes hire young people to stock shelves and handle inventory.

What this could lead to: Some careers that may come out of your time as a warehouse worker include inventory manager, business administrator, truck driver, store manager, product development specialist, and production line supervisor.

Recycle Away

A recyclable material collector is the one who deals with paper, cardboard boxes, plastics, glass, tin, and aluminum items that can be reprocessed. Here's what's involved in a recycler's job:

✧ Collect containers of presorted items and load them into trucks or large bins

✧ Sort through materials in bins to be sure they're all recyclable

✧ Bundle binfuls of material, using crushing and wrapping equipment

✧ Organize bundles for pickup and delivery to recycling plants

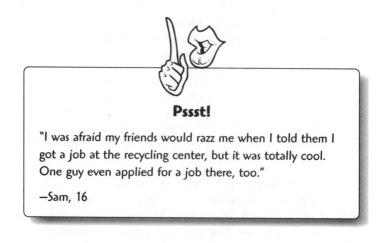

Pssst!

"I was afraid my friends would razz me when I told them I got a job at the recycling center, but it was totally cool. One guy even applied for a job there, too."

—Sam, 16

Not only is this job very PC, it's essential to the well-being of our environment. Almost every community has a recycling service that's either incorporated into its garbage pickups or stands alone as a recycling center where people take their recyclable waste.

What it takes: An interest in recycling is extremely helpful in this job. You'll be dealing with all types of materials, so a curiosity about those materials and how they break down will make your job an interesting one. You'll also need physical strength for all the lifting and hauling you'll be doing. And you'll need to be alert and have good eyesight to spot any unrecyclable stuff that may have found its way into large recycling containers.

Where the jobs are: Check with your garbage service to see if it needs help on its local recycling pickup route. Look in your Yellow Pages to see if there's a recycling center near you. And then inquire at companies (like bottling companies, plastics manufacturers, and newspaper publishers) who might have so much waste that they have their own recycling setups.

What this could lead to: You might enter the field of environmental science, renewable energy, or waste management as a result of your time as a recycler. Or you may turn to a career in hauling, trucking, furniture moving, or garbage removal.

Wash 'n' Wax

Carwashers (or vehicle washers) usually work in teams to clean dirty vehicles ranging from Miatas to MAC trucks. In most cases, here's what a carwasher does:

- ✧ Hoses down the car
- ✧ Scrubs the exterior of the car using cleaning agents, brushes, and cloths
- ✧ Dries and waxes the exterior
- ✧ Vacuums and cleans the interior
- ✧ Operates drive-thru carwash equipment
- ✧ Collects money (sometimes including tips) and gives change to customers

Inside Dope

For more information about what vehicle cleaners do, check out the International Carwash Association Web site (www.carwashes.com).

If you're into witnessing the transformation of cars from grime to shine, this is the job for you. You'll also see customers' faces brighten at the sight of their spiffy vehicles when you're done with them. That can be pretty cool, too.

What it takes: Carwash employers look for job seekers who are courteous, reliable, meticulous, and cheerful. To do this job, you can't be afraid of getting your hands dirty or being sprayed by a wild hose (actually, that might feel good on a hot day). You need good teamwork skills and the ability to follow instructions. A basic knowledge of cars wouldn't hurt, since customers are likely to turn to you with questions like,

101

"Why doesn't my radio work after the antenna got ripped off during the carwash?"

Where the jobs are: You're apt to find work as a carwasher at by-hand and drive-thru carwashes, usually located on busy streets. You might also check commercial transportation companies such as trucking services, bus companies, and taxicab services to see if they need help in their private carwash operations.

What this could lead to: From this job, you might go on to become a truck driver, auto mechanic, car salesperson, auto production line assembler, vehicle designer, or public transportation professional.

Hop to It

Bellhops get paid to carry other people's stuff at hotels, motels, and resorts. It's a straightforward job that entails ...

◈ Greeting travelers when they arrive.

◈ Carrying bags to their rooms.

◈ Delivering ice, food, or messages to guests.

◈ Bringing bags from the guests' rooms to their cars when they check out.

An attractive feature of this job is the tips. Even small tasks like delivering food to a guest's room is likely to land a buck or two in your pocket.

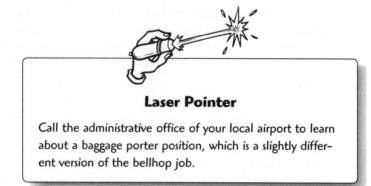

Laser Pointer

Call the administrative office of your local airport to learn about a baggage porter position, which is a slightly different version of the bellhop job.

What it takes: Reliability and a friendly disposition are really important, especially if you're hoping to get tips on this job. You also need to be strong and organized since you may find yourself multitasking. (Picture yourself unexpectedly needing to help Mr. Dunnow operate the elevator, while on your way to deliver ice to Miss Keeto at the pool, and then deliver Mrs. Carriyon's luggage that was delayed at the airport three hours ago.)

Where the jobs are: Apply for bellhop jobs at hotels, motels, vacation resorts (how does Club Med sound?), cruise ships, and fancy bed-and-breakfasts.

What this could lead to: If bellhopping is a hit with you, you might end up in a hotel management position, or in the delivery business as a courier or office administrator.

The Picky Farm Worker

Fruit and vegetable pickers work seasonally. That could mean picking one type of produce after another as it becomes ripe in your area (for example, if you live in North Carolina you might pick peaches in June, corn in July, and tomatoes in August), or chasing harvests around the country (you could pick Florida strawberries in April, pick California avocados in August, dig Maine potatoes in September, and pick New York apples in October). In any case, here's what the work's likely to entail:

✧ Using hand tools such as shovels, trowels, hoes, shears, knives, and clippers

✧ Picking, cutting, or digging fruits, vegetables, or nuts

✧ Sorting and discarding damaged produce

✧ Packing and loading harvested produce

This work is labor-intensive and is usually performed in the bright sunlight, so get ready to have a ravishing suntan (wear your sunscreen!).

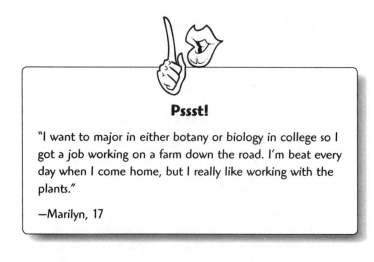

Pssst!

"I want to major in either botany or biology in college so I got a job working on a farm down the road. I'm beat every day when I come home, but I really like working with the plants."

—Marilyn, 17

What it takes: You must be physically strong and in good health (how's your back?). Endurance is necessary, as is the ability to do repetitive tasks such as picking a particular vegetable all day for many days in a row. Teamwork also comes into play, especially on large farms where there are a number of workers on the harvesting crew.

Where the jobs are: This one is obvious: on farms, in orchards, and in greenhouses. To get the contact information for picking opportunities, call your state employment agency and read the Help Wanted ads in your newspaper.

What this could lead to: You might get inspired to become a farmer, botanist, plant illustrator, environmentalist, or herbalist.

Move Over, Buddy

A mover works for a moving company that transports furniture and other goods from one location to another. Movers work in teams to ...

✧ Pack fragile items into boxes.

✧ Remove drawers and strap furniture doors shut.

✧ Carry boxes and furniture out of the building.

> ✧ Load items onto the truck using packing materials to protect items during transit.
>
> ✧ Drive the truck to the destination.
>
> ✧ Unload pieces and carry them into the new building.

Some moving companies specialize in commercial work (like moving a business from one office building to another). Others target residential customers, which could involve local or cross-country moves.

What it takes: Muscles, muscles, muscles! And by the time you've done this for a month, you'll have even more muscles. A logical mind for moving awkward objects around corners and up and down stairs is extremely useful. Following directions and being a good teamworker are absolutes (imagine yourself and a buddy carrying a big glass cabinet down three flights of winding stairs).

Where the jobs are: Unless you have a relative in the moving business who can give you a job, look in the Yellow Pages for a moving company you'd like to work for.

What this could lead to: You might find you like driving big vehicles and decide you want to become a professional truck driver or bus driver. Other options include managing your own moving or hauling company, or working in public transportation administration.

Working Out Even More

Despite all the automation we have around us, there are plenty of jobs that require hard labor. Here are 10 more ideas for using your muscles:

Auction runner	Farm and ranch animal handler
Baggage porter	Mason's helper
Debris hauler	Merchandise shipper
Ditch digger	Plumber's helper
Electrician's helper	Tree cutter's helper

The Mosh Pit

Don't rule out one of the jobs mentioned in this or other chapters in Part 2 because of your gender. All of these jobs can be performed by either sex, so go for any that appeal to you.

Do any of these make your heart rate go up? If so, see if you can find a place to get paid to do one of the workouts on that list.

The Least You Need to Know

✧ Manual labor can be extremely satisfying to those with a desire to stay in shape and a love of hard physical work.

✧ Landscape helpers and groundskeepers get to work outside with lawns, plants, and garden tools.

✧ Jobs that involve a lot of heavy lifting include construction helper, warehouse worker, recyclable material collector, and mover.

✧ To get paid to be outdoors in the sun, look for a job as a deckhand or a fruit or vegetable picker.

✧ If you love working with cars and making them shine, take a job as a carwasher.

✧ As a bellhop, you incorporate your physical strength with your customer service skills.

Chapter 7

You Got Skillz!

In This Chapter

✧ How skills increase your earning power

✧ What's the deal with computer-related jobs?

✧ What it takes to get into printing

✧ Putting it together as a carpenter or painter

✧ Getting down and dirty with cars

✧ Cooking your way to success

Good skills equal good money. In the job market, your skills translate into value when applied to the right job. And the more complicated the task you perform, the bigger your paycheck.

Okay, we're not talking rocket science, but you do need some brain power and skill to do the jobs described in this chapter. Some are computer-intensive (tap, tap); others involve tinkering with cars (zoom!) or food (yum!). No matter what the subject, these jobs all require concentration and, all together now: attention to details!

How Did You Get Here?

You probably landed in this chapter for one or more of the following reasons:

1. You circled 1a, 2a, 3a, 4a, 4b, or 5a on the "You've Got Personality" quiz in Chapter 2, "Your M.O. at Work."

2. You like and do especially well in science, language arts, tech, or music and the arts in school.

3. You're reading through all the job descriptions in Part 2, "Top Fifty Jobs," to see which ones pique your interest.

4. You're curious to learn what jobs might lead to a career you want to pursue.

The Mosh Pit

Skilled jobs don't pay a load of money in the beginning, but if you end up following one through to a career, you're apt to be making a bundle.

This chapter will give you the lowdown on the following 10 skilled jobs:

Computer programmer	Printing press operator
Web site developer	Painter's helper
Graphic designer	Carpenter's helper
Word processor	Auto service technician
Data-entry keyer	Cook

As with all entry-level jobs, you're likely to start at minimum wage and move up from there. Computer-oriented jobs tend to start out a little higher than the rest mentioned in this chapter. Other factors that make a difference include who you're working for, where you live, and the level of your skill.

Read on to see which skilled jobs spark your interest.

Writing in Code

Computer programmers create and refine computer applications, scripts, and more. No one is expecting someone in his or her teens to program KRALL supercomputers, but if you know the basics of even one of the following systems and programming languages, you may fit right into a job as a junior programmer:

- ✦ C/C++
- ✦ Visual Basic
- ✦ Perl
- ✦ Java scripts
- ✦ UNIX or LINUX

In any entry-level spot, you'll be supervised by a more experienced programmer, which is a great way to learn real-world skills. You'll probably be assigned to a group (the JAVA script group or UNIX shell group, for instance) that'll take advantage of your skills. You may find yourself testing software and recommending fixes.

What it takes: This is detail-oriented work that requires someone who thinks logically and sweats the small stuff. In addition to programming, any special abilities (like designing or troubleshooting) will make you stand out.

Where the jobs are: Check out companies in your area that develop computer games, educational software, or business applications for desktop publishing and spreadsheets. Also, inquire at small, medium, and large companies to see if they need help developing programs that are customized for them.

Inside Dope

Here's a hot Web site that lists high-tech jobs: www.dice. com. Scan through it to see which jobs are at your skill level and in your part of the country.

What this could lead to: Those who start out as computer programmers often find themselves immersed in their work and want to make a career out of it. If that's the case with you, consider one of the following professions: computer scientist, computer engineer, systems analyst, database administrator, or Web site developer.

Ze Webmeister

Web site developers create images, text, and graphics that grab a Web surfer's attention. They also do nuts-and-bolts work that keeps Web links working. That means ...

✦ Writing in HTML.

✦ Working with HTML editors.

✦ Creating layouts.

✦ Proofreading text and graphics on screen.

That's a wonderful mix of creative and technical skills, which gives the developer an immediate sense of gratification seeing his or her ideas come into full color on the screen.

What it takes: Creating Web pages takes patience and diligence. You'll be checking and rechecking your work, and keeping track of changes. Accurate typing skills and comfort with computers are essential, as is experience with the Web.

Where the jobs are: Just about every company and nonprofit organization hires someone or a team of people to develop and maintain their Web sites. Depending on your skill level, you could apply to a small company where you might be on your own with the Web site; or go to a large company where you could fit into a team as a junior member.

Laser Pointer

If there's a nonprofit organization you or your family is already hooked into (maybe your synagogue or a civic group), check to see if you could be paid to create or update its Web site.

What this could lead to: Web designers with experience are naturals for the top spot of Webmaster, which is someone who's in charge of an entire Web site. Or, if you pick up some other computer languages and applications, you could become a computer programmer, systems analyst, IT manager, or graphic designer.

Be Graphic

Graphic designers (also called commercial artists) use their artistic skills to create marketing materials for employers such as corporations, retail stores, and advertising or design firms. Here's what graphic designers do:

✧ Design promotional displays and marketing brochures for products and services

✧ Develop distinctive company and product logos

✧ Create visual designs of annual reports and other corporate literature

To do these projects, graphic artists use design software such as Photoshop to generate new images and then create layouts using other software such as PageMaker and QuarkXPress.

What it takes: You need artistic and technical abilities, period. Get your best work together to create a strong portfolio to show to potential employers (if yours is an online portfolio, all the better). While some artists still do design work manually, most perform their wizardry on computers these days. Training or certification programs in computer graphics can certainly help your resume.

Where the jobs are: The places that hire graphic artists include advertising agencies, newspapers and magazines, commercial print houses, and large companies with in-house creative departments.

What this could lead to: Graphic designers can become art or design directors, freelance designers, or Web designers. Some do illustrations for magazines, or go into related fields like photography, interior design, and art teaching.

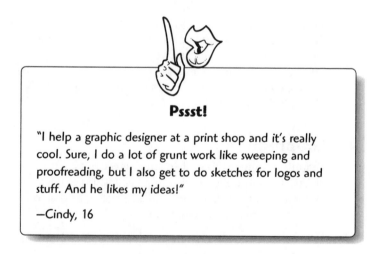

Pssst!

"I help a graphic designer at a print shop and it's really cool. Sure, I do a lot of grunt work like sweeping and proofreading, but I also get to do sketches for logos and stuff. And he likes my ideas!"

—Cindy, 16

Word Processing Whiz

Word processors type. If that doesn't sound like much, just look at what kinds of things they do!

✧ Prepare reports

✧ Write letters

✧ Create mailing labels

✧ Type headings on form letters

✧ Prepare standard forms on typewriters and computers

In addition to keyboarding duties, word processors often do other office tasks, such as answering telephones, filing, and operating copiers and other office machines.

What it takes: Typing quickly (at least 50 words per minute) and accurately is most important, as is good spelling, punctuation, and grammar skills. Any familiarity you have with standard office equipment (like faxes and copiers) and procedures (like alphabetizing and filing) will help you slip right into the groove on this job. Familiarity with a word processing application is a huge plus when going for this job.

Where the jobs are: Wherever there's an office, there may be a need for a word processor. Here are likely places to find such job openings: private businesses (such as insurance companies and law firms), schools, government agencies, and medical offices.

What this could lead to: It's common for word processors to be promoted to administrative assistants, office managers, and supervisors of word processing departments. Others (like me) move into freelance writing and end up authoring books.

Details and Data Entry

Data-entry keyers do a lot of detailed typing. Unlike word processors, data-entry keyers often use database software such as Excel, FileMaker, or a customized database application. Here's what their work entails:

✧ Typing lists of items, numbers, or other data into computers

✧ Completing online forms

✧ Editing current information

✧ Proofreading new entries

The Mosh Pit

Data–entry keying isn't for everyone, even those with good typing skills. It takes someone with meticulous work habits to keep all the details straight.

The data that a keyer enters could be customers' personal information (age, sex, etc.), medical records, and membership lists. In addition to typing on desktop computers, many keyers use a machine that converts the information they type to magnetic impulses on tapes or disks for entry into a computer system.

What it takes: Employers generally hire candidates who can type at a decent speed and with a high degree of accuracy. Spelling, punctuation, and grammar skills are important, and familiarity with office work helps. Any knowledge of word processing, spreadsheet, and database management software is a bonus.

Where the jobs are: There's a big demand for data-entry keyers, whether it's in government agencies or companies that do accounting, auditing, and bookkeeping. Other possibilities include banks, and computer and data-processing services. Personnel agencies (listed in the Yellow Pages) can be very helpful in finding you a job in this field.

What this could lead to: This work frequently serves as a stepping stone to higher paying jobs with increased responsibilities. It's possible for a data-entry keyer to move up to other clerical positions, such as statistical clerk, supervisor of a data-entry department, or database manager.

Punch In at the Print Shop

Printing press operators prepare, operate, and maintain the printing presses in a pressroom. This work involves ...

✧ Installing and adjusting the printing plate.

✧ Inking the press.

✧ Loading paper and setting the press to the paper size.

✧ Monitoring press operation.

✧ Making adjustments to correct uneven ink distribution, speed, and temperatures.

Inside Dope

To get more info on printing and graphic arts jobs, go to these Web sites: Graphic Communications International Union (www.gciu.org) and the Graphic Artists Information Network (www.gain.org).

In most shops, a press operator also serves as Mr. Fix-it, oiling and cleaning the presses and making minor repairs. Junior press operators generally load, unload, and clean presses.

With time, they move up to operating one-color, sheet-fed, or web offset presses and eventually advance to multicolor presses.

What it takes: You must be comfortable working with machinery, and should be able to communicate effectively and take directions. This kind of work has lots of procedures that have to be followed to the letter, so be prepared to learn quickly. Math skills are a plus, and any computer knowledge is good, since newer presses are computerized. Courses in chemistry, electronics, color theory, and physics are helpful, as is an eye for color.

Where the jobs are: Some copy centers hire first-time print workers to run offset printers. Large companies with in-house printing departments often take on junior workers. Printing plants that produce magazines, reports, stationery, or business cards are ideal places to look for work.

What this could lead to: Printing press operators who get interested in the printing industry may become print production professionals, climbing the ladder from junior press operator to first pressman in charge of a printing team. They may also become managers or branch out into print sales. Or they may develop their technical skills and get employed in the growing online market of Web site development, online book distribution, print-on-demand publishing, or distance learning.

Prime Painter

Painters' helpers (or painters' apprentices) apply paint, stain, varnish, and other finishes to the surfaces of buildings. They may work inside or outside, on residential or commercial structures, depending on the assignment. Their work includes ...

- ✧ Choosing the right paint or finish for the surface to be covered.

- ✧ Stripping, sanding, and wire-brushing old coats of paint.

- ✧ Washing walls and trim to remove dirt and grease.

✧ Applying a primer or sealer to prepare surfaces for the finish coats.

✧ Using brushes, rollers, and spray equipment to apply new finishes.

The Mosh Pit

When looking into painting assignments, ask about ventilation on the job. Outside jobs are no problem. But if you'd be painting inside, you want plenty of ventilation since even water-based paint is unhealthy to inhale.

Most painters learn the trade informally on the job as a helper to an experienced painter. Trainees carry supplies, erect scaffolds, and do simple painting and surface preparation while they learn the ins and outs of painting.

What it takes: As an apprentice or helper you may need to be at least 16 years old and in good physical condition. You should have dexterity and a good sense of color. Interest in math will help a lot because there's lots of measuring and calculating to be done.

Where the jobs are: The first place to start looking for this kind of work is with painting and paperhanging companies. Other places to look include local government (property maintenance department), construction firms, real estate companies, and property management agencies.

What this could lead to: Painters may advance to supervisory or estimating jobs with painting and decorating contractors. Many establish their own painting and decorating businesses.

Crafty Carpenter

Carpenters' helpers (or carpenters' apprentices) don't just make birdhouses. They do so many things it's hard to list them all, but here's an idea:

◇ Cut, fit, and assemble wood and other materials

◇ Measure, mark, and arrange materials

◇ Use hand and power tools

◇ Join materials with nails, screws, staples, and adhesives

◇ Check the accuracy of their work with levels, rules, plumb bobs, and framing squares

Pssst!

"My dad's a carpenter and I've hung out in his shop all my life. I want to get a job away from home this summer so I'm looking for a carpenter's assistant job someplace around Chicago."

—Jesus, 17

As an apprentice, you may also help experienced carpenters do a variety of installation and maintenance work. They may replace panes of glass, ceiling tiles, and doors, as well as repair cabinets and furniture.

What it takes: High school courses in carpentry, tech, mechanical drawing, and general mathematics are good things to put on a resume for this job. You will need to be good with your hands, well coordinated, and fit. Being a quick study and having a good head for numbers also counts.

Where the jobs are: The best place to become an apprentice is with a local carpenter. Other potential employers include construction, masonry, stonework, flooring, and plastering companies.

What this could lead to: Carpenters can become construction supervisors or general contractors. Some carpenters choose to work independently, building substantial residential and commercial carpentry businesses.

Grease Monkey

Auto service technicians do minor inspection, repair, and maintenance to cars and trucks. Under the direction of auto mechanics, they may be asked to ...

✦ Change or add oil in customers' vehicles.

✦ Replace, rotate, and check air pressure in tires.

✦ Perform lube jobs.

✦ Change headlights and windshield wiper blades.

✦ Charge batteries.

✦ Pump gas.

After a little on-the-job training, a new auto service tech can expect to be making simple repairs and helping a mechanic with more complicated jobs.

What it takes: For trainee jobs, employers look for people with strong communication and analytical skills. Because you'll be talking to car owners about their beloved wheels, you'll need to be a people person. Math and computer skills are valued. You must be comfortable with tools and not afraid to get your hands dirty. Feeling at home with machines and knowing more than the basics of combustion engines is a strong foundation for success in this job.

Where the jobs are: To find this sort of job, go to your local car repair shops, auto supply stores, and new- and used-car dealers. Also, some gas stations employ auto service techs.

Laser Pointer

If you intend to pursue a career in auto mechanics, you should apprentice under someone who's really good. Ask people in the car business who's the best in town and see if you can work for that person.

What this could lead to: Learning how to repair and service motor vehicles can lead to more complicated work, like diesel mechanics, body repair, customizing, repair service estimations, motorcycle, boat, and small-engine repair. Other occupations this could grow into include vehicle salesperson, auto insurance agent, and commercial transportation professional.

Flipping Out

Cooks prepare meals in places such as restaurants, cafeterias, and food-delivery companies. This is often fast and intense work which, depending on how large the kitchen is and how many employees work there, could involve ...

✧ Weighing and measuring ingredients.

✧ Cooking batches of food.

✧ Stirring and straining soups and sauces.

✧ Cleaning, peeling, and slicing vegetables and fruits.

✧ Making salads.

✧ Baking breads, pastries, and desserts.

In a large operation, you might start out as assistant to the chef. In smaller kitchens (such as a mom-and-pop diner), you might begin as a short-order cook.

What it takes: Basic food handling, preparation, and cooking skills are necessary in this position. Commercial kitchens, even those with only a few workers, must operate as a team in order get food out quickly. That means you need to be able to coordinate tasks with others, and in some cases you may be asked to manage other kitchen workers (such as choppers and stirrers) in food prep. Good math skills are necessary for understanding and multiplying recipes, and a solid knowledge of kitchen safety is essential.

Where the jobs are: Restaurants and cafes are a sure bet, as well as hospitals and schools. You could also try the deli or meat department of your local grocery stores.

What this could lead to: Some cooks move into their own businesses as caterers or restaurant owners. Others become teachers in vocational programs in high schools, community colleges, or other academic institutions. And some go on to become executive chefs or managers in hotels, clubs, and elegant restaurants.

Laser Pointer

Even if you don't fall into a career as a chef, your experience as a cook will serve you well because: 1) you can fall back on your kitchen skills if your primary career goes sour; and 2) you'll always have friends, since people love people who cook good food!

More Smart Work

Now that you've got a feel for skilled jobs, which ones can you picture yourself doing? Maybe you need a few more suggestions, such as:

Baker	Medical and scientific illustrator
Cartoonist	Photographer's helper
Costumer's helper	Stage set designer
Fashion illustrator	Wallpaper hanger
Floral designer's helper	Window dresser

This list could go on and on. If you're still stumped, try thinking of what special skill you have and would like to develop into a paid position.

The Least You Need to Know

✧ If you have a special skill or are interested in developing one, consider a job that highlights that skill.

✧ Jobs that involve using computer skills include computer programmer, Web site developer, graphic designer, word processor, and data-entry keyer.

✧ Those who have excellent dexterity should consider a job as a printing press operator, painter's helper, or carpenter's helper.

✧ If you love working with cars and trucks, go for a job as an auto service tech.

✧ Cooks have one of the hottest jobs in town—and they can make good money at their work.

Part 3

Nailing Down the Job

You know what kind of job you want but you don't understand how to hook up with one. Should you wander the streets and take the first job offered you? Probably not! Will a stranger knock on your door and suggest you come work for her? I don't think so! Or will a parachute fall from the sky and drop a job application into your backpack? Oh, right! All three possibilities are unlikely. You're probably going to have to go out and find a job on your own.

In this part, you'll learn the best ways to find and land a job. In some cases that could mean doing a little paperwork. But hey, you're used to that from all the homework you've got under your belt. And this paperwork will be a cinch 'cause I'm going to tell you what to say in your resume, cover letter, and job application. And then I'm going to explain how to pull off an awesome interview.

Chapter 8

Go Find an Employer

In This Chapter

✧ Knowing what safety issues to look out for at a work site

✧ Finding a job at a totally cool company

✧ Schmoozin' your network to find a job

✧ Using the newspaper and employment agencies to find work

Remember the last time you heard about a hot CD and you just *had* to have it right away? What did you do? You went out and bought it! And if you didn't know which store sold it, you did a little digging, got the name of the store or Web site, and went for it.

Now that you know what kind of job you want, you need to find a place that will hire you to do that kind of work. You got it—you need to go find your employer!

This chapter tells you how to use your low- and high-tech skills to size up whether you want to work for a company.

Safety First

Before considering a job, you want to make sure that it's going to be a safe place to work. A safe work environment has ...

✧ Good ventilation.

✧ Sufficient lighting.

✧ Temperature control (heater or air conditioning if necessary).

✧ Ergonomically sound furniture (for instance, chairs and desks that promote good posture).

✧ Emergency equipment (for example, fire extinguisher, telephone, and first-aid kit).

Unsafe things a young person should never be asked to do on the job include ...

✧ Operating power equipment (such as forklifts and meat slicers).

✧ Working at dangerous heights (for example, on roofs or scaffolding) or depths (such as in mines or deep under water).

✧ Making direct contact with electrical power.

✧ Traveling in unknown or high-risk neighborhoods, especially late at night.

✧ Working alone in a cash-based operation (for instance, convenience stores and gas stations).

✧ Accepting "under the table" wages (meaning, pay that does not get reported to the federal and state governments and therefore is illegal).

If an employer asks you to do any of these things as part of a job you're considering, don't accept the job! No matter what the pay or how cool the job seems, any of these issues could threaten your safety or cause you a lot of grief.

The Mosh Pit

Want to know what Uncle Sam says are the five worst teen jobs? Visit www.natlconsumersleague.org/worstjob.htm.

Finding Good Company

Now that you know what kind of person you want to work for and you know what safety issues to look out for in a work environment, it's time to go find your ideal job. There are five ways to do that:

✧ Apply to a particular company

✧ Network

✧ Respond to ads

✧ Go through an employment agency

✧ Search online

Let's look at how to do each of these.

That Special Gig

Landing a job doesn't have to involve a lot of work. You might already know of a company or organization that you'd love to work for. Maybe you've been fantasizing about working in a particular store that's really cool; or you'd die to get a job at a certain company because its products kick butt. If so, cut to the chase and do the following:

1. Call, write, or walk in to the business and ask to speak to the manager (or to a human resources person if it's a large company).

2. Explain that you'd like to work there.

3. Ask what the hiring procedure is ('cause you'd like to get on board ASAP).

Laser Pointer

Even if you're not looking for a job right now, make a list of companies you'd like to work for sometime (you might hear of one on TV, a friend might tell you of one, or you might like a business whose products you use). Then when it comes time to find a job, you can run down your list of employers.

The employer will love your enthusiasm and will probably hand you an application form right away. Having made such a confident impression with Ms. Employer, you're bound to be considered for a job. And if there isn't an opening now, she'll probably file your application away for future reference.

Schmoozin'

There's an old saying: It's not what you know, it's *who* you know. That axiom is often true in the job market, especially when you're looking for your first job.

So think long and hard (make a list) of all the people you know who might know someone (who might know someone else) who could lead you to a job.

✧ Does one of your parents or relatives know of a job? (Maybe there's a receptionist job opening in your aunt's office.)

✧ Do any of your parents' friends know of an available job? (Maybe your dad's best friend has a summer job opening on his construction team.)

✧ Does one of your teachers have a lead on a job that would complement your studies? (Maybe Ms. Francais knows of a messenger position that's open at the French Consulate.)

✧ Does a friend have previous experience at a company and he or she could recommend you for a job there? (Maybe your basketball buddy used to be a salesperson at Sports R Us and he could turn you on to a job there.)

✧ Are there professionals in your life who might point you in the direction of a job? (Maybe your dentist has connections at the dental school where she teaches and could deliver your resume for a clerical position.)

In other words, call everyone you know and ask them if they know of someone you could talk to about a job. The name of the game is networking, and it's a skill you'll need for the rest of your career. So look at this job search as an opportunity to learn the art of networking (otherwise known as schmoozing).

Pssst!

"I'm really shy and I hated the idea of networking for a job. The idea of walking up to a stranger terrified me. I was relieved to find out that I already had a network: my friends and relatives. They were easy to talk to."

—Randy, 16

Pounding the Streets

As you go about your daily business (going to school, skateboarding, hanging with friends), remember that you're on a mission: You're looking for your employer. Keep your eyes open at all times for the following:

✧ Help Wanted ads in the newspaper

✧ Signs in storefront windows that ask for job applicants

Make a habit of checking the classified section every day. Skim through the various categories to see if there's something that catches your eye. Using a highlighter or ballpoint pen, circle those that appeal to you. Then pick up the phone and say the magic words: "I'm calling about your ad for a [whatever] position listed in the paper."

When you see a sign in the window of a company you think you might want to work for, go for it! If you're dressed pretty decently, just walk in and ask for a job application. If you wouldn't be caught dead by an employer in what you're wearing at the moment, take note of the address where you saw the sign and come back later when you look better.

Call Your Agent

Check the Yellow Pages to find an employment agency that represents the type of work you're after. When you call the agency, ask the following three questions:

1. Do you place people in jobs in the [whatever] line of work?

2. What's the process of applying for jobs through your agency?

3. Do you charge the applicant a fee for your services?

There are three types of employment agencies: for-profit, nonprofit, and government-run. For-profit agencies get paid by companies to find candidates to fill particular job openings. Nonprofit and government-run agencies list jobs for no fee to the employer; their goals are simply to improve society by reducing unemployment. Whether you go through a for-profit, nonprofit, or government-run agency, here's what you can expect it to provide:

✧ A listing of available jobs

✧ Job descriptions and wage expectations

✧ Contact information for employers, unless the agency makes the initial contact for you

Employment agencies may test you for your job skills (like a typing test for a word processing application). If the word "test" makes you quiver, remember this: Testing will help you figure out whether or not you're suited for the job, and, if you do well on the test, it will give you extra confidence when you start on the job.

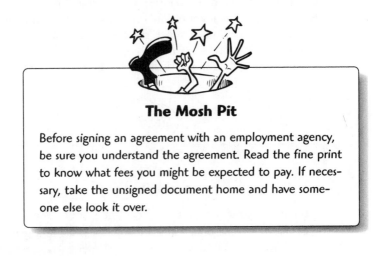

The Mosh Pit

Before signing an agreement with an employment agency, be sure you understand the agreement. Read the fine print to know what fees you might be expected to pay. If necessary, take the unsigned document home and have someone else look it over.

Online Search

Most job Web sites list career-type jobs for workers in their 20s or older. There are, however, some that are more suited to your summer or after-school job search. In addition to the Web sites mentioned in Part 2, "Top Fifty Jobs," check out these:

✧ The Riley Guide Seasonal, Temporary, and Kinda Cool
Work Options
(www.dbm.com/jobguide/msc.html#summer)

✧ Jobstar Summer Jobs
(www.jobstar.org/adjobs/index.htm)

✧ Entry Level Job Seeker Assistant
(www.dnaco.net/~dantassi/jobhome.html)

✧ Seasonal and Summer Employment
(dir.yahoo.com/Business_and_Economy/Employment_
and_Work/Jobs/Seasonal_and_Summer_Employment/)

✧ gotajob.com (www.gotajob.com)

✧ Summer Jobs for Teenagers
(www.bygpub.com/books/tg2rw/summer-jobs.htm)

Also, conduct your own Web site search. Open one of your
search engines (my favorites are Lycos and Hotbot) and enter
keywords (such as "sales, shoes, summer jobs") into the
browser window, and see what job ops appear on your screen
(maybe a cool job selling sandals on the beaches of Bermuda).

Inside Dope

Be sure to go to your state employment agency's Web site
or visit its real-life office (info listed in Appendix A, "Agencies That Work") to see what jobs are offered in your area.

What's Next?

Using the suggestions in this chapter, you're bound to find
an employer you want to work for. Once you find him or

her, you need to apply for the job. If your application requires a resume, turn to Chapter 9, "Resumes That Rock." If it needs a cover letter, go to Chapter 10, "The Big Cover-Up." When you need help filling out your application form, read Chapter 11, "Blankety-Blank Applications."

The Least You Need to Know

✧ Before taking a particular job, be sure that its work environment is a safe one.

✧ If there's a company or nonprofit organization that you'd love to work for, go ahead and ask for a job there.

✧ There may be someone in your network of friends and family who knows of a job for you.

✧ Keep your eyes peeled for Help Wanted signs in store windows and check the classifieds in the newspaper for a job.

✧ Consider going through an employment agency to find work.

Chapter 9

Resumes That Rock

In This Chapter

✧ Figuring out if you need a resume

✧ Looking deep to know what to write about

✧ Getting a handle on resume formats

✧ A step-by-step guide for each section of your resume

Resume ... that's just French for "A sheet of paper that says 'here's why you should hire me for the job.'" When a prospective employer asks you for a resume, you'll need to know how to put one together.

In this chapter I'll lead you through the resume-writing process from rough draft to finished copy. I promise you, this is peanuts compared to some of those projects they've hit you with at school! Just stay with me on this and we'll come up with an impressive one-page resume.

Who Needs a Resume?

A lot of after-school, weekend, and summer job applications don't require resumes. For most of the jobs mentioned in

Part 2, "Top Fifty Jobs," you'll be able to walk into the place of business, pick up an application form, sit down for an interview, and snag the job.

But you might run into a situation like one of the following that requires a resume:

✧ You see a sign in a window that says something like, "Sales Associate Wanted. Send Resume."

✧ You spot a Help Wanted ad in the newspaper that asks for a resume.

✧ You want to apply for a job that's kind of far from home so you need to send a resume and cover letter (see Chapter 10, "The Big Cover-Up") to make a good impression.

✧ You're trying to get into a college that expects a resume to accompany the application form.

✧ You learn of an internship (see Chapter 16, "Inside Internships") you want at an institution that requests a resume as part of its application process.

If you don't need a resume for the job application you're working on now, you don't have to read this chapter. In fact, you can jump ahead to Chapter 11, "Blankety-Blank Applications." But someday you probably *will* need a resume, and the following info will come in handy.

Believe It or Not

If this is a first for you, you may think you've done nothing noteworthy to put down on paper, much less something that would impress an employer. "I don't have any experience!" you insist. Look again! I'll bet you've had a lot of work experience that you may not have gotten paid for.

Think about what you've actually got under your belt for life experience. You've undoubtedly done a scary amount of school-related projects and activities in addition to what you've had to do at home. You may even be able to list some volunteer work.

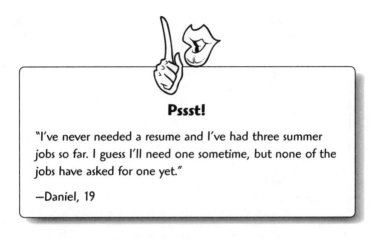

Pssst!

"I've never needed a resume and I've had three summer jobs so far. I guess I'll need one sometime, but none of the jobs have asked for one yet."

—Daniel, 19

Take a look at what some of your compadres listed as work:

✧ Andrea grew up next to a dog kennel. She loved the dogs and would help out whenever she could.

✧ Glen's mother ran a home daycare center. He dealt with safety issues and helped think up ways to occupy the toddlers.

✧ Jose learned a lot about politics while convincing the principal of his high school that there wasn't adequate parking.

Of all the many things you've done in your life, which ones can you squeeze into the category of "experience"?

You've Got Style

There are two resume styles: functional and chronological. Like most job seekers your age, you should use the functional resume style since it highlights skills you've developed through your varied activities (paid or unpaid). Later in life, when you have more paid experience under your belt, you may decide to use the chronological format.

Here's a template for the functional style, followed by Ben E. Fishal's functional resume.

(Functional Resume Template)

Name
Street
City, State Zip
Phone
E-mail

JOB OBJECTIVE
    The job you want

SUMMARY OF QUALIFICATIONS
- Explain that you have experience either doing the job mentioned in your job objective or using some of the skills required for that job.
- Tell what aspect of your personality is particularly suited for this job.
- Mention one of your school or extracurricular activities that supports this job objective.

RELEVANT EXPERIENCE

MAJOR SKILL
- Describe an accomplishment you're proud of that required this skill.
- Briefly describe a problem you solved using this skill, and tell the results.
- Talk about a time when you used your skill to positively affect someone.
- Mention an award you received that shows you have this skill.

MAJOR SKILL
- Talk about a project you worked on using this skill.
- Write about an accomplishment that shows you have this skill.
- Describe a time when someone "sat up and took notice" of your skill.

WORK HISTORY

200x-present	Job Title	Company name and city
200x-xx	Job Title	Company name and city
200x-xx	Job Title	Company name and city

EDUCATION
    Current Class, School, City, State
    Relevant courses (optional)

COMMUNITY SERVICE

Your volunteer title (current or past)	Name of organization
Your volunteer title (current or past)	Name of organization

Functional resume template.

Ben E. Fishal
4 Infomashion Highway
Overwhelm, ND 12345
123-555-1234
benefishal@thescene.com

JOB OBJECTIVE
Web site designer for teenink.com

SUMMARY OF QUALIFICATIONS
- Experience designing Web sites using GoLive and PhotoShop.
- Understand the interests and attention spans of teens on the Web.
- Spend more than three hours a day on my computer and the Net.

RELEVANT EXPERIENCE

Web Site Design
- Designed www.fiscalfishal.com for my father's small business, using GoLive for Macintosh.
- Revamped my school's Web site, adding an animated slide show to generate more interaction with students.
- Developed and maintain my site (www.yotalk.com) that targets the teen audience and gets about 150 hits a week with no advertising.
- Mentioned on www.webbies.com as a contributor to the site's content.

Computer Skills
- Helped seven Power Mac users upgrade to G4s, installing new software and peripherals on each system.
- Team-taught computer classes (PCs and Macs) at the adult education center.
- Known as "the Web dude" among friends.

WORK HISTORY

School year 2000-01	Web Designer (part-time)	Fiscal Fishal, Inc., Overwhelm
Summer 2000	Salesperson	Hard Wired, Overwhelm

EDUCATION
Senior, Poweron High School, Overwhelm, ND
Relevant courses: Computer Programming, Web Design

COMMUNITY SERVICE
Assistant Computer Instructor, Overwhelm Adult Education

Sample functional resume.

Now that you have a sense of what a resume looks like, let's tackle the job of creating one for you.

Inside Dope

For more information on how to write a functional or chronological resume, read my book, *The Complete Idiot's Guide to the Perfect Resume* (published by Alpha Books, 2000), or go to my Web site at www.susanireland.com.

Top Info

The first thing to appear on your resume is your heading: your name, followed by your address, phone number, and e-mail address (if you have one). Each piece of information should be on a separate line; and you can put them in the center or right side of the page, whatever you think looks best.

Job Objective with Direction

A few spaces down from your heading, write "Job Objective:" followed by the type of work you want to do. If you haven't figured out what kind of work you're going after, review Chapter 2, "Your M.O. at Work," and the job descriptions in Part 2.

Stating a job objective near the top of your resume helps Mr. Busy Employer determine right off the bat what you're looking for so he won't have to read through the whole resume and then guess what job you want.

Take a peek at Ben E. Fishal's resume (earlier in this chapter) to get an idea of how to word your job objective. Notice that Ben's is concise—not a vague, long-winded sentence referring to growth opportunity, work challenge, or any of that fluff.

It's to the point: just the name of the job he's looking for. That's how you want to deal with yours.

The Mosh Pit

Don't put your name in the upper-left corner of your resume. It's more effective if it's in the center or right-hand side of the page. You see, when the employer puts your resume in a file folder, the left side of the page is apt to be in the spine of the folder. If your name is on the left, it won't be seen easily.

Summing It Up

The next section of the resume, called "Summary of Qualifications," is a cinch. It's just three short bullet-point lines stating why you'd be good at the job you're going for. To come up with some good one-liners, ask yourself the following questions.

Brainstorm for Your Summary Statements

1. How much experience do you have in this type of work or in using the required skills?

   Sample answer from Sylvia, who's going for a nurse's aide position: *Well, I've never worked in a hospital, but I helped take care of my grandmother when she was really sick last year. And I help my mom take care of my younger sisters and brother when they get sick.*

   Sylvia's summary statement: *Experience assisting in the care of sick children and adults.*

Your summary statement:

_____

_____

_____

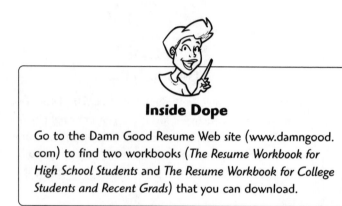

Inside Dope

Go to the Damn Good Resume Web site (www.damngood.com) to find two workbooks (*The Resume Workbook for High School Students* and *The Resume Workbook for College Students and Recent Grads*) that you can download.

2. What coursework or credentials do you have that are important for this job?

   Sample answer from Bob, who's seeking a lifeguard position for the summer: *I took the Red Cross course in CPR this spring and I got my lifeguard certificate last winter.*

   Bob's summary statement: *Certified lifeguard with recent CPR training.*

   Your summary statement:

   _____

   _____

   _____

3. What is it about your personality that makes this job a good fit for you?

   Sample answer from Reid, who's after a job as a researcher: *I love solving mysteries and have an endless curiosity that drives me to find the answers to questions.*

   Reid's summary statement: *Intense curiosity to dig up information and answer questions.*

Your summary statement:

_____

_____

_____

4. What extracurricular activities or interests do you have that would be valued by the employer?

Sample answer from Page who wants to be a proof-reader for a teen publication: *I love to read; I read everything I can get my hands on. I've done it since I learned how when I was six and I especially like reading articles about social trends.*

Page's summary statement: *Avid reader with special interest in the social impact of teen trends.*

Your summary statement:

_____

_____

_____

Not all of these questions will work for your situation. That's okay! Just answer the ones that do, and you're bound to come up with a few good statements for your "Summary of Qualifications" section.

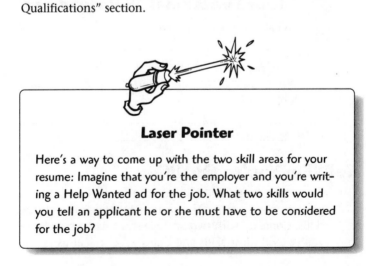

Laser Pointer

Here's a way to come up with the two skill areas for your resume: Imagine that you're the employer and you're writing a Help Wanted ad for the job. What two skills would you tell an applicant he or she must have to be considered for the job?

Skills for Sale

The next section on your resume is called "Experience." It's the body of your resume where you'll tell what experience, paid or unpaid, you have that supports your job objective. And because you're writing a functional resume, you're going to categorize your experience according to the skills you'll use on the job you're seeking.

Usually there are two most important skills needed to do a job. When asked to say what two skills they will use most on their jobs, here's what two job seekers said:

Leonora, age 16, wants an office job that she can go to for a few hours after school, Mondays through Fridays. She thinks project management and word processing will be essential for that job.

Perry, age 19, believes his skills at motivating others and working with kids will come in handy as a guidance counselor for juvenile offenders.

What two skills will you need most for the job mentioned in your "Job Objective" section?

Your Functional Skill Headings

1. What's your job objective?

   _____

   _____

2. What are the two skills required to perform your job objective?

   _____

   _____

Tell 'Em You're Qualified

For each of those two skills you just wrote down, think about projects where you've demonstrated that you have those skills. Come up with two or three short sentences that say you've used those skills and that you're *good* at using them.

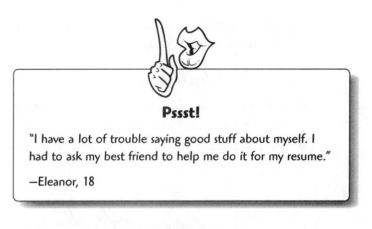

Pssst!

"I have a lot of trouble saying good stuff about myself. I had to ask my best friend to help me do it for my resume."

—Eleanor, 18

Here's how Leonora presented her skills and achievement statements on her resume for an after-school office job:

Project Management

✧ Organized my class's first scooter relay as a fundraiser for the March of Dimes.

✧ Planned my family's vacation activities once we got to Atlantic Beach last summer.

Word Processing

✧ Word processed six school reports last year, each ranging from four to seven pages long.

✧ Served as a teacher's assistant to the after-school computer program for middle school kids.

Perry, who was applying for a job as a guidance counselor for juvenile offenders, wrote the following on his resume.

Motivation

✧ Reduced student tardiness by starting a before-school hip-hop contest in the gym to get kids to arrive at school early.

✧ Came up with the "Cool kids don't smoke" slogan, used throughout the school.

Work with Kids

✧ As camp counselor at Lake Winnakid, taught children ages seven through sixteen to swim.

✧ Assisted in leading backpacking trips in the Pocono Mountains for young adults with disabilities.

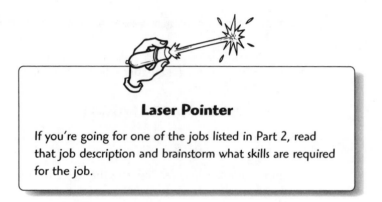

Laser Pointer

If you're going for one of the jobs listed in Part 2, read that job description and brainstorm what skills are required for the job.

Now use the following worksheet to write statements for your skill headings. Not all of the questions will work for your situation. Just answer the ones that do.

Brainstorm for Your Experience Statements

1. Have you used the skills you'll need for this job in a previous situation? Describe it.

   Sample answer from Bill, who would like a job as an accountant's assistant: *For two years now I've helped out in the adult ed computer classes at Sanford High School.*

   Bill's experience statement under the skill heading "Computer": *Assisted computer instructor in adult education classes at Sanford High School for two years.*

Your experience statement:

_____

_____

_____

2. Give an example, from your own life, of PAR (Problem, Action, Result). Name the problem; tell what action you took to correct it; and say what the result was.

Sample answer from Angel, 17, who's looking for work as a preschool teacher's assistant: *Once I was babysitting for a neighbor and the two kids started fighting over a toy. It got serious, with fist fighting and everything. So I separated the two kids, got them each to say to the other one what was bothering them, and helped them work it out without any blood.*

Angel's experience statement that appeared under her resume skill heading "Conflict Resolution": *Resolved conflict between children by listening to each one's point of view and getting them to talk to each other reasonably.*

Your experience statement:

_____

_____

_____

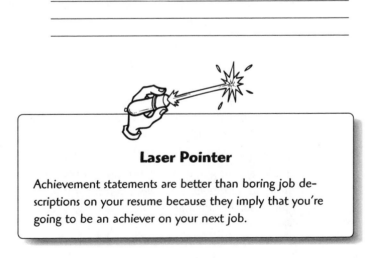

Laser Pointer

Achievement statements are better than boring job descriptions on your resume because they imply that you're going to be an achiever on your next job.

3. When did you use your skill to do something you're really proud of?

   Sample answer from Drew, 16, a high school senior hoping to get an after-school job as a graphic artist: *I was on the high school yearbook staff and did a lot of the illustrations and layout for the yearbook.*

   Drew's experience statement under his "Artwork" skill heading: *Created illustrations and graphic layout for Jefferson High School's yearbook.*

   Your experience statement:

   _____

   _____

   _____

4. Have you won any awards or been recognized for your aptitude in this skill?

   Sample answer from Louis, 17, who would love a job in computer programming: *I got an award at graduation for my proficiency in computer science.*

   Louis's experience statement under his skill heading "Programming": *Winner of a computer science award at high school graduation.*

   Your experience statement:

   _____

   _____

   _____

5. Is there something good you've done for your friends or family that they admire and respect you for?

   Sample answer from Ling, 18, who's applying for a job as a local tour guide for the summer: *I'm the one my friends all turn to for directions, especially if it's a long trip. I love reading maps and figuring out the best route to anywhere.*

Ling's experience statement: *Provided clear directions to novice travelers, many of whom had never been far from home.*

Your experience statement:

_____

_____

_____

Education Made Simple

The "Education" section is the easiest of all. Here's what to put in it:

1. The name of the high school you're attending. If you just graduated, put your year of graduation. Otherwise put the class you're in now or, if it's summertime, put the class you'll enter in the fall (freshman, sophomore, junior, or senior).

2. If you'll be going to college in the fall, don't put your high school down as mentioned in #1. Just write the name of the college and the class (freshman or sophomore) that you'll be entering in the fall.

3. List any special training you've had that supports your job objective. (Maybe the tech you took in school would come in handy for that carpentry job you're after.)

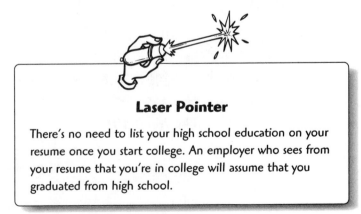

Laser Pointer

There's no need to list your high school education on your resume once you start college. An employer who sees from your resume that you're in college will assume that you graduated from high school.

See how Ben E. Fishal listed his education in the sample resume earlier in this chapter.

Extra, Extra, Read All About It

Here are a few sections that *might* appear on your resume after the "Education" section:

❖ Community Service

❖ Memberships

❖ Personal Pursuits

❖ Computer Skills

Let's look at each of these sections to see which, if any, you need.

Community Service: If you do volunteer work, create a "Community Service" section that adds to your qualifications for the job; or if you think it makes you look like a person with darn good character. (For example, you would say that you were a fundraiser for the Arthritis Society if you're going for a sales position, since both roles involve persuading people to part with their money.)

Memberships: Create a "Memberships" section if you belong to groups outside of school that are directly related to your job. (For instance, you might list the YWCA and Girl Scouts of America if you're applying for an athletic or recreational job.)

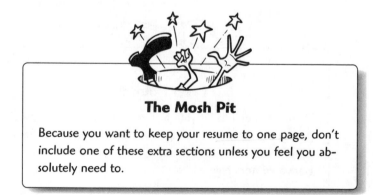

The Mosh Pit

Because you want to keep your resume to one page, don't include one of these extra sections unless you feel you absolutely need to.

Personal Pursuits: Add a "Personal Pursuits" section if you haven't already mentioned some extracurricular activities that make you a special candidate for the job. (For example, the fact that you spent last summer hiking around the Grand Canyon might be of interest to the owner of a travel agency where you're applying.)

Computer Skills: Include a separate "Computer Skills" section only if those skills are highly relevant to the job and you haven't been able to incorporate them into the resume elsewhere. (For example, a list of the languages and platforms you know would be a great section to have on your computer programming resume.)

Each of these sections is simply a laundry list underneath the section heading. Remember, add one of these sections only if there's room on your paper without making it go to a second page and only if it doesn't cramp the layout of your one-pager.

Putting Things in Place

Now that you've figured out what you're going to put on your resume, you just need to pull up a document on your computer and type it in. Use the template found earlier in this chapter to get the order of each section right.

Once you've input all your info, you're ready to print it and proofread it. When you're sure it's perfect, turn to the next chapter, where you'll learn how to write a dynamite cover letter.

The Mosh Pit

Don't let even one mistake appear on your resume. Proofread it very carefully and ask a friend or family member to proofread it as well.

The Least You Need to Know

❖ Your name and contact info should appear at the top of your resume.

❖ Write a brief job objective statement just under your heading.

❖ Create a short "Summary of Qualifications" section that says why you'd be good at that job.

❖ Under "Experience," list achievements that show that you have the skills required for the job.

❖ Your "Education" section appears at the bottom of your resume.

❖ Your resume should fit on one page and should have no misspellings or grammatical errors.

The Big Cover-Up

In This Chapter

✧ Gettin' down with cover letter wording

✧ What's the deal with formatting your letter?

✧ What to say and how to say it

✧ Putting together a reference sheet for your interview

Every conversation needs an ice breaker, especially when it's between people who don't know each other. In the case of your job application, that ice breaker may be a cover letter that accompanies your resume.

This chapter will tell you when you need a letter and how to write it. It's a painless process, so let's get started.

The Word on Cover Letters

Whenever you send your resume by mail or e-mail, you need to include a cover letter—something to introduce that impressive resume you just wrote (see Chapter 9, "Resumes That Rock").

Situations that might call for a mailed resume and cover letter include ...

✧ Applications for jobs that aren't within reasonable driving distance from your home.

✧ Job openings at corporations that have a resume submission process (usually through their human resources department) that applicants are expected to go through.

✧ Internships that require resumes and cover letters as part of their formal applications (see Chapter 16, "Inside Internships," to learn more).

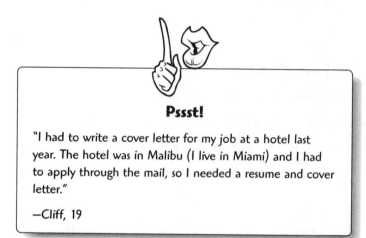

Pssst!

"I had to write a cover letter for my job at a hotel last year. The hotel was in Malibu (I live in Miami) and I had to apply through the mail, so I needed a resume and cover letter."

—Cliff, 19

If none of these apply to you, then you probably don't need a cover letter. That means you can jump ahead to the next chapter on job applications.

Since you're still reading, I assume you must need a cover letter. Great! First, let's talk about good cover letter writing technique. Then we'll move on to how to write a letter step by step.

Less Is More

You're going to love this concept: Less is more. When it comes to the guts of your cover letter, the shorter the better, as long as it does the job of introducing you.

I'm talking about three short paragraphs that say ...

✧ What job you're applying for.

✧ Why the employer should want to interview you.

✧ How much you appreciate his or her time reading your letter.

✧ When you'll call to see about an appointment for a job interview.

Even though that may sound like a mouthful, it's not. In the next few sections you're going to learn how to say it in a straightforward, natural way that will be quick and easy for the employer to read.

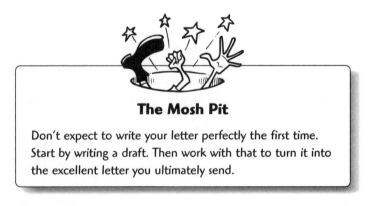

The Mosh Pit

Don't expect to write your letter perfectly the first time. Start by writing a draft. Then work with that to turn it into the excellent letter you ultimately send.

Be Yourself

Here's my big cover letter tip: Show attitude (positive attitude, that is!). In other words, don't try to write an overly formal letter that sounds like something you pulled out of a book (like the one you're holding right now). Don't use phrases that sound canned, like "Enclosed please find my resume for [whatever] position." That's not the way you'd talk to someone, so don't write that way.

Instead, use a casual yet polite style that shows you'd be an interesting and even fun person to interview—and to have working at the company.

Notice the friendly yet respectful tone in A. Ford D'Amusik's cover letter.

A. Ford D'Amusik
4A Song Circle
Emm, NM 12345
123-555-1234
tap2damusik@screech.com

April 8, 2001

Ms. Carrie Toone
Boomin' Music
One Disc Drive
Emm, NM 12345

Dear Ms. Toone,

I've been a regular customer of Boomin' Music for the last three years. I probably spend more hours looking through your CDs than Britney Spears spends in front of the camera. With school letting out for the summer, I wonder if you'd need another salesperson to handle the extra business.

I work well with people, and I think that with my knowledge of bands and singer-songwriters, I'd be a good salesperson. And I already know how your stock is organized in the store.

I'd like to come in and talk to you about my working at Boomin' Music. I'll call you within the week to see if we can set up a time for that. Thanks for reading my resume and considering my qualifications.

Sincerely,

A. Ford D' Amusik
Enclosure: resume

Sample cover letter.

Get Going

Now that we've discussed good cover letter writing strategy, let's get started on your letter. The next steps will take you from top to bottom of your masterpiece. As you read the steps, look at the following template to see exactly where each element of the letter goes. It couldn't be easier!

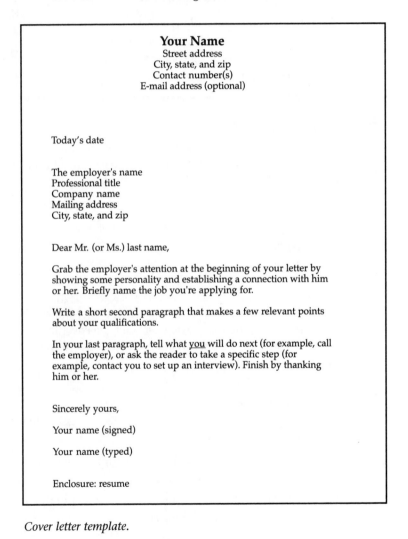

Your Name
Street address
City, state, and zip
Contact number(s)
E-mail address (optional)

Today's date

The employer's name
Professional title
Company name
Mailing address
City, state, and zip

Dear Mr. (or Ms.) last name,

Grab the employer's attention at the beginning of your letter by showing some personality and establishing a connection with him or her. Briefly name the job you're applying for.

Write a short second paragraph that makes a few relevant points about your qualifications.

In your last paragraph, tell what you will do next (for example, call the employer), or ask the reader to take a specific step (for example, contact you to set up an interview). Finish by thanking him or her.

Sincerely yours,

Your name (signed)

Your name (typed)

Enclosure: resume

Cover letter template.

The Mosh Pit

Even though your letter looks formal with its letterhead and inside address, it should not sound formal. Give it a conversational tone by using contractions and appropriately casual language.

Step One: A Head Start

Since you've already gone through the step of creating a heading for your resume, why go through that work all over again for your letter? Instead, let's rip it off! Here's how:

1. On your computer, make a copy of your resume.

2. Name your new document "Cover Letter."

3. In the Cover Letter document, delete everything except the heading.

There you go—you've got letterhead that's ready for the contents of your letter. By the way, to see how this and the following steps pan out on paper, check out the cover letter template and sample letter that appeared earlier in this chapter.

Step Two: Inside Info

Now you're ready to write the date and inside address. Follow these steps:

1. Put your cursor immediately below your heading and space down a few lines.

2. Type today's date (for example, June 13, 2001) so that it starts on the left side of the page.

3. Skip down a few more lines and type the employer's name, title, company, and address (each on a separate line).

4. Leave one line blank and then type your salutation (for example, Dear Ms. Demeanor).

Turn to the template that appears earlier in this chapter to see exactly how these three elements are laid out.

Step Three: For Starters

The first paragraph should say something catchy like ...

✧ How you learned about the job.

✧ The name of the person who referred you to the man or woman you're writing to.

Opening phrases should be upbeat and even chatty. Show the employer you've got spunk by writing something like one of the following:

"Last week's *River Journal* popped out at me when I saw your picture on page 17C."

"Hally Tossis mentioned that you're looking for an assistant in your dental office. I'd like to apply for that position."

"Last year, you came to my school to give a presentation on teen crime. I was the one in the third row who asked about recent legislation."

See what I mean? Be yourself: polite, interesting, and energetic.

Step Four: Make Your Point

The second paragraph should be brief and make one or two points such as ...

✧ What job you'd like (if you haven't already said that in your first paragraph).

✧ What you have to offer on this job (maybe you could mention what talents you bring to the table that are particularly suited for this employer's company).

✧ A hint of what you'd like to talk about in the job interview (maybe you'd like to learn more about a certain aspect of the job).

Here are three examples of good second paragraphs:

"For years I've been seen as a really persuasive guy (I campaigned hard for that new skateboard park that was put up just outside the emergency room of St. Mary's Hospital). I'd like a shot at using my persuasive skills as a member of your sales team this summer."

"With the rise in cell phone sales, I imagine you could use a friendly person to answer your customers' technical questions. As a cell phone junkie, I know I could do the job."

"I'd love to work in your office as an assistant to your executive assistant. I've been taking computer classes in school and I'm eager to put my new skills to use."

No need to go on and on in this part of your letter—two or three sentences are plenty.

Inside Dope

You can find sample cover letters on my Web site (www. susanireland.com) and in my book *The Complete Idiot's Guide to the Perfect Cover Letter* (published by Alpha Books, 1997).

Step Five: Thanks a Lot

The third paragraph is your closer. Muster all your courage to say ...

✥ You'll call the employer (if you have the phone number) to see when you can come by for an interview.

✥ You appreciate the employer's time in reading your letter.

Here are three sample closing paragraphs:

"Thank you for taking the time to read my letter and resume. Friday, June 2, isn't a school day and I'd be free to come in for an interview. I'll call your office in a few days to see if that works for you."

"I appreciate your taking the time to read this. Would you be able to speak to me sometime next week about the sales job? I'll give you a call to see when is good for you."

"I'd like a chance to talk with you in person about exactly what's involved in your office work. Is there a time next week when I could come by? I'll call in a few days to check with your secretary. Thank you for considering me for the job."

Now that you've got the hang of writing good content for your letter, it's almost time to sign your name.

Step Six: Signing Off

You're almost done—just a few quick steps left:

1. Write your complimentary close (something like "Sincerely," "Sincerely yours," or "Thank you!").

2. Skip down a few lines (where you'll later sign your name by hand).

3. Type your first and last names.

4. Below your name and flush left, write "Enclosure: resume."

To see these steps in action, refer to the template earlier in this chapter.

Laser Pointer

When your letter is finished, the print should take up no more than 50 percent of the whole page. The other 50 percent (including the top, bottom, and side margins) should be white space.

Reference Ready

When you go for your job interview, you should take a sheet that lists your references on them. References are people who have agreed to talk to potential employers and to put in a good word for you. (For a brush-up on how to get employment references, refer to Chapter 1, "What's So Cool About Having a Job?") Your references could be ...

✧ One or more teachers.

✧ A religious leader.

✧ A former employer.

✧ An adult friend.

✧ An organizer of a club you belong to.

Ask four or five people if they'd be job references for you, and then put together your reference sheet like this:

1. Create a new document for letterhead the way you did for your cover letter. (Follow the steps under "Step One: A Head Start" earlier in this chapter.)

2. Space down a few lines and type each reference person's name, title (meaning his or her relationship to you), address, and phone number—each piece of information on a separate line.

3. Prioritize your list of four or five references so that your number-one reference comes at the top.

4. Leave one or two blank spaces between each block of reference info.

Check out the following reference sheet for Shirley.

Shirley U. Jest
24 Laffin Lane
Confusin, ME 24128
(207) 555-2940

Mr. Willie Work
(my former supervisor)
West Wing Chicken Express
1255 Wealthy No. Way
Poore, ME 24128
(207) 555-3647

Ms. Betty Wont
(my English teacher)
Hardly High School
145 Hooky Highway
Confusin, ME 24128
(207) 555-9382

Mr. Justin Time
(family friend)
235 Gonna Drive
Confusin, ME 24128
(207) 555-4930

Mr. Tad Toolate
(my softball coach)
335 Cottona Circle
Confusin, ME 24128
(207) 555-2236

Sample reference sheet.

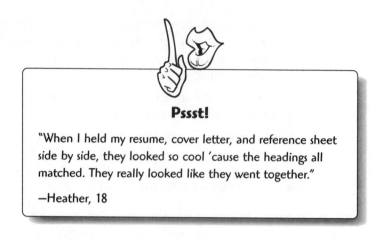

Pssst!

"When I held my resume, cover letter, and reference sheet side by side, they looked so cool 'cause the headings all matched. They really looked like they went together."

—Heather, 18

In Good Shape

You're in excellent shape to mail out your resume and cover letter. And when you get your first appointment for an interview, you'll be ready with your list of references.

The Least You Need to Know

✧ Create letterhead for your cover letter by copying the one you made for your resume.

✧ Keep your letter short, friendly, and respectful.

✧ Place today's date and the employer's name and address below your heading.

✧ Start your letter with a grabber: Mention the name of someone you and the employer both know, or say how you learned about the job opening.

✧ Your second paragraph should give a hint of what you have to offer and what you'd like to talk about in the interview.

✧ Close your letter with a "thank you" and the suggestion that you meet with the employer for a job interview.

Chapter 11

Blankety-Blank Applications

In This Chapter

⟡ Where to get an application form once you know what job you want

⟡ How to fill out your form point by point

⟡ Special tips on tricky parts of the application

⟡ What to do when you return your form to the employer

You've spotted a specific job you want and you're ready to go for it. Now what? You've got to take the big step of applying, and that usually means filling out an application form.

A lot of people draw a blank when it comes to filling out forms of any kind. If you suffer from this problem, don't worry. This chapter will show you how simple it is to get your application form, fill it out, and hand it in. Let's get going!

Picking Up the Ap

One of the easiest ways to get an application is to walk into the place of business where you want to work and ask for the form. Most likely the receptionist will either hand you one or send you to the human resources department (if the company's large enough to have an H.R. department) where a clerk will give you a form.

If you don't live close enough to the business to get the form in person, call the company and ask to have an application mailed or faxed to you. In some cases, a company may refer you to its Web site where you can download a form (or even fill it out online).

Some employers, especially those with small businesses or ones who are desperate to fill positions, may ask you to sit down for an interview when you go in to pick up the application form. Although that doesn't usually happen, it *might,* so prepare yourself for a spontaneous interview by reading Chapter 12, "Ace That Interview," and putting on an interview-type outfit before you head out to pick up your application form.

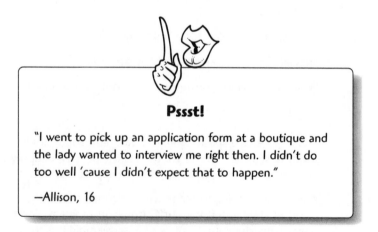

Pssst!

"I went to pick up an application form at a boutique and the lady wanted to interview me right then. I didn't do too well 'cause I didn't expect that to happen."

—Allison, 16

Hopefully the employer won't ask you for an interview on the spot and you'll be able to take the application home. That way you'll have lots of time to think through your answers and print them neatly.

Applying Yourself to the Form

Although it's pretty obvious what to write in most of the spaces on your application form (like your name, date, and phone number), let's go over a few that might throw you for a loop:

✧ **Social Security number.** If you have a Social Security number, write it in this blank. If you don't have one yet, turn to Chapter 13, "You, the Law, and the IRS," to find out how to get one.

✧ **Present address** and **permanent address.** If you intend to live at home while you're working, these two addresses would be the same: your home address. But let's say you're living at a private high school or a college at the time you apply for a summer job. In that case, put your school address for present address, and your home address for permanent address.

The Mosh Pit

Don't turn in an application form that has stuff crossed out. To prevent that from happening, make a copy of the form before you fill it out so you have a backup if needed.

✧ **Salary desired.** Put "minimum wage" unless you know that your experience and skills warrant more pay, in which case, put down the amount you feel you deserve.

✧ **May we contact your employer?** If you're currently employed and don't want your boss to know you're looking elsewhere for a job, write "no." If it's okay for your boss to know you're looking, put "yes."

✧ **Major subjects.** There's no need to put anything under this heading for grammar school. For high school and college (if you've started college), mention a few classes that are relevant to the job you're going for. (Some of the job descriptions in Part 2, "Top Fifty Jobs," mention subjects that are valued for those job applications.)

✧ **GPA.** No need to fill in the GPA (grade point average) space for grammar school, but you should put it down for high school and college, even if it's not a 4.0.

✧ **Subjects of special study or research work.** This is a great section because you can put down any of your extracurricular activities that support your job objective. For instance, if you're applying for a job as a short-order cook, you might put down that you learned all about nutrition at summer camp last year ("Nutrition class at Camp Yum Mee, Summer 1999").

✧ **Special training.** Once again, this is a great chance to talk about any nonschool classes you've taken that make you qualified for the job. For example, someone wanting to be a lifeguard could list his or her CPR class through the Red Cross ("Red Cross CPR Certification").

Inside Dope

Before going to a company to ask for an application form, go to its Web site (if it has one), click on the recruitment or career link, and see if it has an application e-form.

✧ **Activities.** Here's another opportunity to show that you're ready for the type of work you're applying for.

Tell the employer about any volunteer, sport, and other activity you do that's relevant to the job. Or as a way of telling the employer, "Hey, I'm a nice person," you might explain that you put in time at the Salvation Army ("Volunteer donations collector, Salvation Army").

✧ **Former employers.** This is pretty straightforward: If you've never had a paid job, leave this section blank. If you've been employed, even for odd jobs (for example, "neighborhood VCR/TV repairs"), fill it in.

✧ **Salary.** Say how much per hour you were paid at your previous jobs.

✧ **Reason for leaving.** If you left a job on good terms, say "End of summer vacation," "End of assignment," "Wanted to broaden my experience with another job," or whatever is true for you. If you were fired from your last position, say what happened, framing it in a positive light: "Not a good fit," "Left by mutual agreement," or "Agreed to move on." In other words, don't say: "Hated my boss" or "Got fired."

✧ **References.** This is a very important part of the application. Read the "For Future Reference" section in Chapter 1, "What's So Cool About Having a Job?" and the "Reference Ready" section in Chapter 10, "The Big Cover-Up," to learn how to generate a list of references.

✧ **In case of emergency, notify** .... Put the name of your parent, guardian, or other adult who's authorized to make decisions on your behalf in case of a medical or other emergency.

✧ **Are you under 18?** Give a simple yes or no answer. The employer wants to know because if you're under 18, you may need a work permit to qualify for the job (see Chapter 13 to learn how to get a permit).

✧ **Have you ever been convicted of a crime (or felony)?** You must answer this question honestly. If you've ever been convicted of a serious crime (such as rape, murder, assault, or battery), then by law you must say "yes" to this question on your application. Less serious offenses such as parking tickets and running red lights don't need to be mentioned.

That brings you to the end of the application. Just sign your name, add today's date, and you're ready to turn it in to the employer.

Inside Dope

To find out more on how to fill out a job application, read *How to Get a Job If You're a Teenager,* by Cindy Pervola and Debby Hobgood (published by Alleyside Press, 2000).

Turning It In to the Boss

You've filled out your form and you're ready to turn it in. Before you do, ask a smart friend or relative to proofread it for you. He or she should look for ...

✧ Whether or not you answered the questions appropriately.

✧ If there are any mistakes in spelling, grammar, or accuracy.

If you pass both of these tests, you're ready to zip it off to the employer. You can do that in one of the following ways:

✧ E-mail it if you originally got it from the company's Web site.

✧ Fax it.

✧ Send it by snail mail.

✧ Send it via a delivery service like FedEx.

✧ Take it to the company in person.

If you choose the last option, wear something appropriate for an interview and be prepared to meet the hiring manager (see Chapter 12) in case the boss wants to have a sit-down interview with you right then and there.

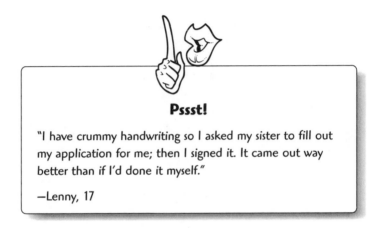

Pssst!

"I have crummy handwriting so I asked my sister to fill out my application for me; then I signed it. It came out way better than if I'd done it myself."

—Lenny, 17

The Least You Need to Know

✧ To get an application form for a specific job, either go to the company and ask for one, call the human resources department to get one faxed or mailed, or go online to download one.

✧ Fill out the form at home, if possible, so you can clearly think through each answer and not make mistakes.

✧ Everything on your application form must be completed fully and honestly.

✧ Ask someone to proofread your completed form for mistakes or poor grammar.

✧ Once the application's filled out, return it to the company.

Chapter 12

Ace That Interview

In This Chapter

✧ Looking good for the interview

✧ Saying the right thing the best way

✧ Asking questions for your benefit

✧ Talking paychecks, perks, and other particulars

Your job interview doesn't have to be nerve-racking. With
just a little planning, you'll step into it as naturally and confi-
dently as Mark McGuire steps up to bat. That fearsome person
pitching you the interview questions is probably very nice.
In fact, there's a good chance that person remembers what it
was like to be in your shoes and will try to make the whole
thing go as quickly and smoothly as possible.

This chapter will get you through your interview without
bruising your self-esteem. In fact, you might even walk away
with a job offer. Are you ready for that? Then follow me!

Dress to Suit

Whether you dress up or down for your job interview depends on what sort of job you're going for. Here's a good rule of thumb: Dress one notch above what you'd wear to a typical day on the job. In other words, if you're applying for work in an office where you'd wear khakis on a daily basis, delve into your "Limited" wardrobe and come up with a casual suit for the interview. If you're going for a job selling surfboards at the beach where you'd wear shorts and a T-shirt to work, put on a pair of nice jeans (no rips or stains) and a casual shirt for the interview. Got it?

Keep Your Foot Out of Your Mouth

"Appropriate" is the operative word when it comes to knowing what to say and how to say it to the interviewer. From "Hello, I'm Andy Fudgeswell" to "Goodbye Mr. Paysgood," you want to show that you're the perfect candidate for the job.

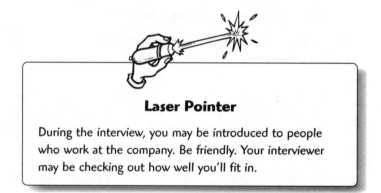

Laser Pointer

During the interview, you may be introduced to people who work at the company. Be friendly. Your interviewer may be checking out how well you'll fit in.

Chances are you already know how to do that, but just in case you have some gaps in your know-how, here's a basic list of do's and don'ts:

✦ Smile, especially when you first meet the interviewer. That good first impression will stick in the employer's mind throughout the meeting and after, when you're being considered for the job.

✧ Take a few copies of your resume (see Chapter 9, "Resumes That Rock"), a list of references (see Chapter 10, "The Big Cover-Up"), a pen, and a notebook to your interview.

✧ Don't wear tons of earrings and jewelry (unless you're applying to a piercing salon), gobs of makeup, or an entire bottle of scent.

✧ Offer the interviewer a confident handshake when you first meet. You don't have to break the guy's knuckles, but make a firm impression and show him you're alive and enthusiastic.

✧ Make eye contact when the interviewer's speaking to you and vice versa. That will give him a sense that you're attentive, interested, and personable.

✧ Good posture counts. Don't slouch or use negative body language such as crossing your arms, clenching your fists, twirling your hair, or clutching your backpack. You don't want to appear scared.

✧ Ditch the gum before the interview. Chewing away on a wad makes a poor impression.

✧ Be honest, even if it means admitting that you don't know something. A lie is bound to get you in trouble, whereas your sincerity will always be appreciated.

✧ Use the interviewer's name occasionally during your conversation. If her name is hard to pronounce (like Ms. Zitszinface), practice it before the interview so you can say it easily.

✧ Your interview starts the minute you walk in the front door and lasts until you exit that door. Put your best foot forward from start to finish.

The Mosh Pit

Don't be late for your interview! Get clear directions ahead of time (make a trial run, if necessary) and get there a few minutes early.

Thinking on Your Feet

Let's do a run-through of your interview with this multiple-choice quiz. Choose the answer that best describes what you would do.

Are You Interview Savvy?

1. You arrive at the interview to find that the Big Guy's in a heated phone conversation. You ...

    a. Get out your cell phone and call your mom.

    b. Use the extra time to good advantage by practicing your Tai Chi.

    c. Wait patiently in the reception area.

2. You finally have his full attention. You ...

    a. Call Mom again.

    b. Begin talking feverishly about last night's party.

    c. Shake his hand confidently and sit down.

3. The interviewer offers you coffee. You ...

   a. Ask if it's freshly ground.

   b. Explain at length that coffee drinkers turn you off.

   c. Go for it, unless you know you'd spill it all over yourself.

4. The fire alarm goes off! You ...

   a. Knock him down and drag him from the building.

   b. Throw a chair out the window.

   c. Follow his lead.

5. The interviewer has to leave the room for a while. You ...

   a. Sit in his chair and put your feet up on the desk.

   b. Put a tack on his seat.

   c. Sit patiently, recompose your thoughts, and try not to fall asleep.

6. You think you might have bits of food between your teeth. You ...

   a. Refuse to open your mouth to talk.

   b. Put a bag over your head.

   c. Ignore it (too late).

7. You suspect that the interviewer is reading the wrong application form (he called you by someone else's name). You ...

   a. Get mad and storm out.

   b. Play it out (it could lead to a better job).

   c. Politely reintroduce yourself.

continues

continued

8. The interviewer asks what job experience you've had. You ...

   a. Gasp that you feel an asthma attack coming.

   b. Tell him you've been too busy hangin' out with your friends to work.

   c. Explain how you've gained some of the skills required for the job.

9. There is a long silence. You ...

   a. Start giggling.

   b. Get out your nail clippers.

   c. Let the interviewer deal with it.

10. Part way through the interview, you panic. You think you might not want to work for this guy! You ...

    a. Run.

    b. Start doing the opposite of all you've learned so far.

    c. Finish the interview and keep your options open.

If you answered "c" to all of these questions, congratulations! You're calm, cool, collected, and ready to ace the interview. (If you answered all "a"s or "b"s, you *are* kidding, right?)

Q&A

The obvious thing is going to happen during your short meeting (probably 15 or 20 minutes) with Mr. Employer: He is going to ask you questions. Even though the questions won't be difficult, give some thought ahead of time as to how you're going to present yourself. Here's a list of commonly asked interview questions that you can practice answering. (I've inserted sample answers from teens applying for various types of jobs.)

1. **Why do you want this job?** Sample answer: I'm good with math and I've always been comfortable with people. I get along with my brothers and sisters and their friends. I think I might even want to work on the frontline of an airline company someday. So I thought cashiering at your store would be a good start for that kind of work.

2. **Do you have any experience doing this sort of work?** Sample answer: I've never done this particular job but I've done things like it. For example, I know that as a camp counselor I'll need to be good with kids and be able to handle emergencies. I've done babysitting for a family of three since I was 15 and that's involved a lot of safety issues.

3. **What motivates you to do well?** Sample answer: I like to feel like I'm part of a team and I like to learn as I go along on a project. It also feels good to know that I'm accomplishing something.

4. **What school or extracurricular project are you proud of?** Sample answer: I was on the school baseball team and I was really afraid at first, but I did it. Once I got involved and got over my fear of being the underdog, I loved it! I made friends and had a lot of fun competing. I learned that I'm able to take on stuff.

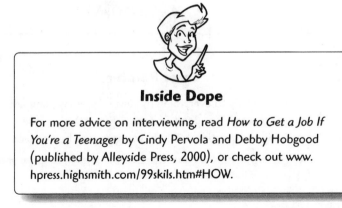

Inside Dope

For more advice on interviewing, read *How to Get a Job If You're a Teenager* by Cindy Pervola and Debby Hobgood (published by Alleyside Press, 2000), or check out www. hpress.highsmith.com/99skils.htm#HOW.

5. **How do you handle conflict? Can you give me an example?** Sample answer: Well, I don't really like conflict so I try to avoid it. If I do have a problem, I try to resolve it before it gets blown out of proportion. For instance, my sister and I always seem to need the car at the same time. We used to argue over who got it every Saturday night until I realized that I needed to plan it out ahead of time so it wasn't an issue when I was about to grab the keys. When it's really important to me, I make a deal early in the week—one she can't refuse like money or doing her jobs for her. Whatever works.

6. **Can you tell me about your work habits?** Sample answer: I don't let myself get bored, so as soon as I'm done with something I look for what else I can do with my extra time. Sometimes that's just cleaning up or organizing my workspace. I like to be productive. I'm also good at working with people.

7. **What are your plans for after you graduate?** Sample answer: I'm going to go to Foothill Community College and then on to The Paul Bunion School of Podiatry. In the meantime, working in the stockroom of your shoe store seems like a good fit.

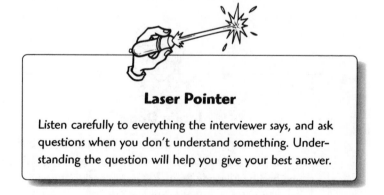

Laser Pointer

Listen carefully to everything the interviewer says, and ask questions when you don't understand something. Understanding the question will help you give your best answer.

8. **What would you do if you saw someone stealing?**
   Sample answer: If it was a customer, I'd go directly to
   my supervisor or the security guard and report it. If it
   was a fellow worker, I'd wait until a private moment to
   talk to you or my supervisor, or maybe I'd talk directly
   to the person. Is there a certain way you'd want me to
   handle it?

9. **What would you do if friends wanted free stuff?**
   Sample answer: I'd just tell them I can't help them. If
   they want discounts on CDs at this store, they should
   get a job here, like I did.

10. **Aside from money, what do you think you'll gain**
    from working here? Sample answer: Experience.
    Friends. I want experience working with technical pro-
    fessionals like the ones who work here. I want to get a
    feel for this line of work and I think I'll probably end
    up making some friends at the same time.

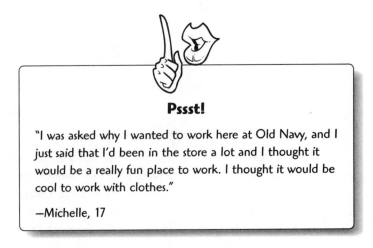

Pssst!

"I was asked why I wanted to work here at Old Navy, and I
just said that I'd been in the store a lot and I thought it
would be a really fun place to work. I thought it would be
cool to work with clothes."

—Michelle, 17

Turning the Tables

The interview process is a two-way street—you get to ask
questions, too. Some of your questions may even indicate to

Mr. Employer that you've done your homework regarding the job you're after. Here are some things you might want to ask:

1. What will be expected of me as an employee?

2. Once I'm on the job, who will I report to?

3. What hours would you like me to work? Will overtime be required?

4. How many days a week would the job involve?

5. About how many people would I be working with?

6. Is there any training needed for the job?

7. How will I know if I'm doing the job right?

8. If I do well, is there a way I could take on more responsibilities?

9. My family is going on vacation the last week of July. Would I be able to join them for part of that time?

10. Will I need to buy uniforms or provide myself with anything special?

Laser Pointer

The employer will usually mention salary, but if she doesn't, don't ask about it until after talking with her about what you'll be doing on the job. It's better to talk about money once you understand the position. Besides, you don't want the employer to think you're in it just for the green stuff.

Be upbeat when you ask your questions. Staying relaxed and positive will in turn put the interviewer at ease and make everything go more smoothly.

Deciding If You Want the Job

Most interviewers won't make you a job offer during the interview. They frequently have other candidates to check out before they choose who they want for the job. If, however, your interviewer springs an offer before you go through the exit door, resist making a final decision *unless* you're sure this is the job for you, in which case go ahead and say "yes." If you're not sure, put off giving an answer by saying something like: "I'm interested in the job and I'm really glad I had a chance to talk to you about it. Could I give you an answer tomorrow?" That way you give yourself time to think it over, consider other options, and get input from friends and family.

The Mosh Pit

If you're unsure of how to answer a question, take your time. It's okay to have a brief moment of silence before you respond. And you know what? The employer may be impressed with your thoughtfulness.

Suck It Up!

Not everyone who interviews for a job gets a job offer. Chances are you're going to run into a rejection here and there, even though you know you're a great candidate. The best way to handle rejection is to realize that, although you're a smart person and a hard worker, the job might not be a good fit for you. If the employer recognizes that, she won't offer you the job.

If she calls you the day after the interview and says: "I've decided to hire someone else," don't fall into a mental mosh pit. There are other jobs out there, and the one you end up with will likely be a better one for you. Keep your spirits up and get out there with your resume again.

But don't mistake silence for rejection. If a couple of days go by after the interview and you haven't heard a word, call the employer to check the status of your application.

Laser Pointer

Have a few job applications in the works in case your first choice doesn't pan out. That way, if number one isn't a winner you can jump right on number two.

Money Talk

Most summer and part-time job offers don't involve heavy pay negotiations. Usually the employer has a wage in mind and that's what the pay's going to be. Depending on the type of work you're doing, you may be paid by the hour (for example, $6 an hour for baby-sitting), by the piece (for example, $1 a T-shirt that you silk-screen), or by commission (for example, 15 percent of each sale that you close as a telemarketer).

Once the employer tells you how much the job pays, you might have some questions, such as ...

1. Am I likely to get tips in this job? If so, do you know approximately how much they would amount to per week?

2. How often would I get paid (weekly, biweekly, or monthly)?

3. Are there bonuses attached to the job? (Some employers of seasonal help offer a bonus for employees who stick it out until the end of the season.)

4. Are there any perks that go with the job? (If you're working at a retail store, maybe you'll get a discount on things you bought there.)

5. What benefits do you provide? (Companies sometimes offer health insurance and, believe it or not, retirement funds, even to part-time and short-term employees.)

Inside Dope

To get an idea of what the going rate is in your area for a particular type of work, go to your state employment Web site and look for its salary and wage surveys. (See Appendix A, "Agencies That Work," for URLs, phone numbers, and addresses.)

The Big Thank You

When the interview is wrapping up, be sure to say "thank you." And to make a big impression, use the interviewer's name—something like: "Thank you, Mr. Gates. I'm glad we had a chance to meet."

On your way out, say "thank you" to the receptionist or security guard, using his or her name, too. It's always smart to make friends with these gatekeepers. After all, you may end up working (or even hanging out after work) with them.

The Least You Need to Know

✧ For your job interview, dress one step up from what you would expect to wear normally on the job.

✧ Before your interview, practice how you'll answer questions the employer is likely to ask, and make a list of questions *you* want to ask about the job.

✧ Make a good impression by smiling, having good posture, making eye contact, and being friendly to everyone you meet at the job site.

✧ Avoid talking about pay until after you understand all that's involved with the job.

✧ After the interview, say "thank you" to the interviewer, as well as to those who ushered you in (such as the receptionist or security guard).

Part 4
You're Hired!

Some people get off on following rules and regulations to a T. Others get a little teed off with the idea of having to read and follow sticky directions. Whichever type of instruction follower you are, you'll want to read this part to be sure you know at least the bare minimum about the job of having a job.

These chapters give answers to questions you might not have known to ask, things like: What governmental forms do I need to fill out? How do I handle employment taxes? What am I supposed to do with my paycheck? The best news is that all this isn't complicated and you can do it!

Chapter 13

You, the Law, and the IRS

In This Chapter

✧ What the federal child labor laws have to do with you

✧ How taxes affect your paycheck

✧ Getting a Social Security number

✧ How to find out if you need a work permit

✧ Filling out W-4, Employment Eligibility, and other government forms

Holding down a job involves dealing with some red tape, things like Social Security numbers, government forms, and taxes. It's nothing you can't handle—you just need to learn how the employment system works with regard to your state and federal governments.

This chapter tells all you need to know about getting registered with the government, obtaining necessary employment papers, and reporting preliminary tax information. With a little care, Uncle Sam's red tape won't seem sticky at all.

A New Relationship

Once you get a job, you need to strike up a new relationship with your state and federal governments. These governments want to know what kind of work you're doing and how much you're being paid for two reasons:

1. They want to be sure you're treated fairly and safely.

2. They want percentages of the amount you earn (otherwise known as taxes).

Let's take a closer look at these two points.

Big Brother's Youth Employment Laws

There was a time in American history when children (anyone under 18, according to the law) were exploited by employers. In some cases, kids were forced to work unthinkably long hours, under terrible conditions, and for extremely low wages. In 1938, the federal government stepped into the workplace with the Fair Labor Standards Act (FLSA), which includes child labor laws. These laws set minimum age, wage, and working condition requirements for workers under 18 years of age. The primary goal of the FLSA child labor laws is to protect you, the young worker.

Inside Dope

To grasp the impact of how the child labor laws affect your employment, go to the U.S. Department of Labor Web site for child labor (www.dol.gov/dol/esa/public/youth/cltour1.htm). It's an easy-to-understand site with an animated slideshow.

Here are the most important aspects of the federal child labor laws:

1. You must be at least 14 years old to be hired for most "real" jobs. Exceptions include jobs such as acting, modeling, occasional baby-sitting, and newspaper delivery.

2. You must be paid at least the federal minimum wage for the hours you work.

3. You must be paid overtime (at least $1\frac{1}{2}$ times your regular hourly rate) for each hour you work beyond 40 hours a week.

4. You must be provided with safe working conditions and you have the right to complain if the job site is not safe.

5. You must not be asked by your employer to perform tasks that the federal government has deemed unsafe for someone your age to do.

6. You have the right to equal employment opportunities regardless of race, color, religion, sex origin, or disability.

7. You have the right to work free of sexual or physical harassment.

Some states have child labor laws that are stricter than the federal child labor laws. In such cases, the state laws supersede the federal laws. To learn about what federal, state, and local employment laws apply to you, check with your state employment agency (listed in Appendix A, "Agencies That Work") or consult your school counselor or principal.

It's All About Money

The second reason you need to establish a relationship with your federal and state governments is for reporting and paying taxes.

Here are the types of tax that you may need to deal with:

1. Federal income tax

2. Social Security tax

3. Medicare tax

4. State income tax

Pssst!

"I hear people talk about taxes and I never understand what they're saying. It all sounds so scary. I guess I'll just ask my dad what to do when I get a job."

—Tina, 16

Not all states charge income tax. To learn if you'll need to pay a state tax, check with your state employment agency (listed in Appendix A) or ask your school counselor, your employer, or any working adult.

Why is it important to know about taxes? Two reasons:

1. You need to pay them. Have you ever heard of tax evasion? That's what you could get charged with if you didn't pay up to Uncle Sam or to your state kitty.

2. It helps you understand how much of your wages you get to keep after your Medicare, Social Security, and income taxes have been taken out.

When an employer tells you you'll make a particular amount per hour, you need to subtract the amount of your state and federal taxes to know how much money will actually land in your pocket. Use this worksheet to calculate your weekly paycheck.

Laser Pointer

If you get tips on your job, keep track of how much you get, because tips need to be reported to the government as part of your income.

Calculating Your Paycheck

Your Weekly Earnings

1. Your hourly wage: _____

2. Number of hours per week you work: _____

3. Your weekly earnings (multiply lines 1 and 2): _____

Your Weekly Taxes Withheld

Tax	Percentage of Tax You Pay	Amount of Tax Withheld (Multiply #3 by the Tax Percentage)
4. Federal income tax	Probably 15%	_____
5. Social Security tax	6.2%	_____
6. Medicare tax	1.45%	_____
7. State income tax	_____	_____
8. Total weekly tax: (add lines 4 through 7):	_____	_____

Your Weekly Paycheck

9. Remainder of weekly earnings (subtract line 8 from line 3): _____

Don't fret about how to pay your taxes. Your employer is going to deduct a certain amount (called a tax withholding) from your earnings, send your withholdings to the federal and state governments on your behalf, and then issue you a paycheck for the remainder of your earnings. You have to complete only a few simple forms before April 15 of the following year.

The Order of Events

Now for the nuts and bolts of getting in gear with your government agencies. Here's a simple to-do list that you can use to check off each step as you complete it.

Your To-Do List

❑ 1. Apply for your Social Security number, if you don't already have one.

❑ 2. Get a job offer.

❑ 3. Obtain a work permit (if required).

❑ 4. Go to your first day on the job.

❑ 5. Show your identification.

❑ 6. Fill out an Employment Eligibility Verification (Form I-9).

❑ 7. Complete an Employee Withholding Allowance Certificate (Form W-4).

❑ 8. Submit your work permit (if necessary).

❑ 9. Apply for an Earned Income Credit Advanced Payment (Form W-5) if you are a working parent and meet the requirements for this form.

We've already talked about Step 2: Get a job offer (Chapter 8, "Go Find an Employer") and Step 4: Go to your first day on the job is pretty obvious. Now let's look at how to accomplish the other steps.

We've Got Your Numba!

Your Social Security number (SSN) is the federal government's code for identifying you. Each U.S. citizen is issued just one number during his or her lifetime, and uses that number on all tax and governmental forms. So even if you change your name (let's say you get married, join a religious sect, or get a sex change), your Social Security number will always identify you as the one and only "you."

The Mosh Pit

Before rushing off to get a Social Security number, check with your parents or guardian to see if you already have one (your parents probably got one for you when you were born or when they opened a bank account for you).

To get an SSN, you need to fill out an Application for a Social Security Card (Form SS-5). Here are the ways to get Form SS-5:

✧ Go online to www.ssa.gov/online/ss-5.htm, where you can download a copy of the form.

✧ Pick up a form at your local Social Security office (listed in the phone book).

✧ Call the federal Social Security office (1-800-772-1213) to get one sent to you.

Once you have the form, fill it out (it's super easy), and return it to your local Social Security office by either delivering it in person or mailing it. You will also need to take or mail certain documents that prove your identity. Those documents will be returned to you along with your new Social Security card. (Yep, you're actually going to get a card that you can carry around in your wallet.) The process takes about two weeks once the Social Security office receives your application and ID.

What's Up with Work Permits?

If you're under 18 and you've already been offered the job you want, go to your middle or high school and ask the guidance counselor or someone in the principal's office if you need a work permit. If your state requires you to have a permit (not all states do), you'll need to have it in hand on your first day of work. And since permits are issued for a specific job, you may need to apply for a new one for each job you take until you're 18 years old.

The fastest way to get a work permit is to go to your school counselor or principal, who will ...

◈ Have the work permit application form.

◈ Help you fill it out.

◈ Send your application to the appropriate government agency.

Laser Pointer

It's important to apply for your work permit *after* you've accepted a job offer because the school counselor will need to know what the job is in order to fill out your work permit application.

Your work permit will come to you via snail mail about two weeks after you send in your application. Yes, that means you may not be able to start a job until the permit arrives. But if that's the law, your employer will understand.

Eligible to Work

There's a very simple federal form called the Employment Eligibility Verification (Form I-9) that your employer will give you to complete. This form is very straightforward—it asks you to write your name and address, and to check a box that states your citizenship status. That's it! The rest of this one-page form is filled out by the employer.

W-4 Form for You

On the first day of your job, the employer will present you with a W-4 and ask you to fill it out. This simple form is sent to the Internal Revenue Service (the tax branch of the federal government, also known as the IRS) by your employer. Based on how you fill out your W-4, your employer will determine how much of your earnings to withhold for your taxes. Periodically, the employer sends the state and federal governments your tax withholdings, which get credited to your tax "accounts." That means that at the end of the year when you calculate your state and federal taxes, you may ...

✧ Not owe any tax if the withholdings covered the exact amount of your taxes.

✧ Need to pay the governments just a little tax if most of it was prepaid by the withholdings.

✧ Get a refund (wow, imagine that check in the mail!) if your withholdings equaled more than your actual taxes.

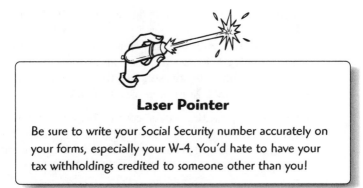

Laser Pointer

Be sure to write your Social Security number accurately on your forms, especially your W-4. You'd hate to have your tax withholdings credited to someone other than you!

The amount that an employer withholds largely depends on how you fill out lines 5 and 6 on your W-4 Form, which read ...

> 5. Total number of allowances you are claiming.

> 6. Additional amount, if any, you want withheld from each paycheck.

Line 5. Here's my advice on how to respond to line 5:

✧ If you are single and your parents or guardians list you as a dependent on their tax forms (meaning that they support you financially), put "0."

✧ If you are single and your parents or guardians cannot list you as a dependent on their tax forms (meaning they do not support you financially), put "1."

✧ If you are not single or if you have children, consult a tax preparer or other knowledgeable adult for advice on what number to put down.

Most teens fall into the first category (single and supported by parents or guardian). Be sure that the information on your W-4 Form agrees with what your parents or guardians put on their tax forms. In other words, if they claim you as a dependent, put zero in line 5 of your W-4. If no one claims you as a dependent, you can claim yourself and thereby pay less tax.

Line 6. Most people leave line 6 blank unless they want the extra security of knowing there's plenty of money in their IRS account to pay their taxes. Putting a dollar amount on line 6 makes sense if you expect you'll get an increase in income through your financial investments, the state lottery, or something like that. Most of us aren't so lucky.

Form W-4 comes with a worksheet that helps you figure out how to fill in the actual form. In addition to using the worksheet, it's wise to get advice from your parents, guardian, tax preparer, or other adult whose judgment you trust.

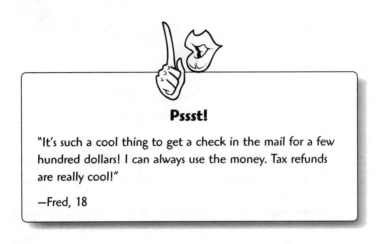

Pssst!

"It's such a cool thing to get a check in the mail for a few hundred dollars! I can always use the money. Tax refunds are really cool!"

—Fred, 18

You're a Mom or Pop

If you're a working parent, you may qualify for certain tax reductions by filling out an Earned Income Credit Advance Payment Certificate (Form W-5). This federal form has only four "yes/no" questions for you to answer. If you meet the requirements stated on the back of the form, you could reduce your tax withholdings, lower your annual tax, and get a refund even if you don't owe any tax. It's definitely worth checking out.

To get a W-5 form, ask your employer, consult your tax preparer, download it from www.irs.ustreas.gov/plain/ forms_pubs/forms.html, or contact the Internal Revenue Service nearest you (found in your phone book under United States Government, Internal Revenue Service, or by logging on to www.irs.ustreas.gov/plain/where_file/california.html to get your local IRS contact info).

The Mosh Pit

Don't be tempted to lie on your government forms in order to reduce your taxes. If you get caught, you could end up paying a fine, and possibly get your records tagged for scrutiny in the future.

The Least You Need to Know

✧ It's important to understand what your federal and state employment laws allow and prohibit with regard to your employment.

✧ To understand how much of your earnings you will keep, calculate the amount of tax you will owe and subtract that amount from your earnings.

✧ You will need to have a Social Security number before you can get employed.

✧ Check with your school to find out if you need a work permit.

✧ On your first day, you will be asked to fill out a W-4, an Employment Eligibility Verification (I-9), and possibly an Earned Income Credit Form.

Chapter 14

Managing All That Dough

In This Chapter

✧ How you think about money and why that makes a difference

✧ Calculating how much dough you have

✧ Figuring out exactly how much cash you need

✧ Devising a plan to afford the stuff you want

Whether you make minimum wage or way more, you want to handle your hard-earned cash like a savvy player who always has money when she needs it. After all, you'd hate to miss out on an outrageous deal on concert tickets just because you were short on cash.

This chapter gives you pointers on how to manage your money wisely without feeling cheap. And if you plan really well, you'll end up with extra cash for the fun stuff.

Getting to Know You

You've probably been getting an allowance for a few years now and have acquired an attitude toward money. Here's a quiz that will tell what spending and saving habits you've already developed.

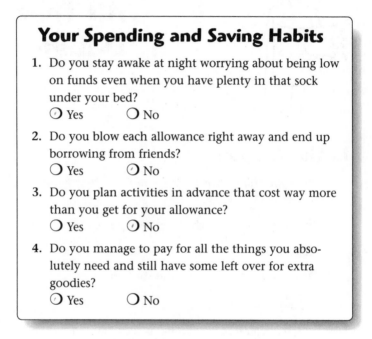

Your Spending and Saving Habits

1. Do you stay awake at night worrying about being low on funds even when you have plenty in that sock under your bed?
   ⊙ Yes   ◯ No

2. Do you blow each allowance right away and end up borrowing from friends?
   ◯ Yes   ⊙ No

3. Do you plan activities in advance that cost way more than you get for your allowance?
   ◯ Yes   ⊙ No

4. Do you manage to pay for all the things you absolutely need and still have some left over for extra goodies?
   ⊙ Yes   ◯ No

Here's what a "yes" answer means for each of those quiz questions.

1. You're probably a conservative spender and a regular saver. This is good, but be careful that you don't become known as a tightwad.

2. You're a big spender and a terrible saver. If this trend continues, you could end up in big debt and without any friends.

3. You're a dreamer who needs to come down to earth. Your unrealistic planning could lead to credit card abuse in the future.

4. You've got a handle on how to manage your dough. Congratulations! Not many people, young or old, have this special talent.

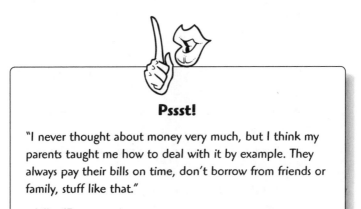

Pssst!

"I never thought about money very much, but I think my parents taught me how to deal with it by example. They always pay their bills on time, don't borrow from friends or family, stuff like that."

—Lilly, 17

What to Do with Your Paycheck

Once you get a job and your first payday rolls around, which of the following will you say to yourself when your boss hands you your paycheck?

✧ Where's the nearest ATM? The mall's open until 9:00 so there's time to spend it all.

✧ If I put the whole thing in my bank account now, I'll be less likely to blow it on things I don't need.

✧ I'll deposit it tomorrow morning after I've had time to figure out just how much I need to save and how much I can afford to spend.

You're in luck—there's no right answer. In fact, how you choose to handle your money will depend on the type of person you are (see the previous quiz, "Your Spending and Saving Habits") and what your immediate financial needs and wants are.

Managing money is a tricky balancing act. You need to save enough to pay for necessities (maybe you have monthly private phone bills and car payments), and have enough left over for extras (like dating and ski trips). To help you figure out how you should distribute your money, let's make two lists: one list of the things you *need;* the other of things you *want.*

You can copy the following blank worksheets and use a clean set to fill out in the following ways:

✧ One for each week of the year, so you can make short-term adjustments

✧ One for each month of the year, so you can make minor adjustments

✧ One for each summer, fall, winter, and spring, to help you plan for seasonal changes such as Christmas spending in winter

✧ One for summer, when you might work full- or part-time

✧ One for the school year, when might have a part-time job

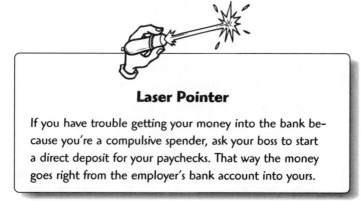

Laser Pointer

If you have trouble getting your money into the bank because you're a compulsive spender, ask your boss to start a direct deposit for your paychecks. That way the money goes right from the employer's bank account into yours.

Because most teens get paid weekly, the following worksheets are based on weekly calculations.

What's Your Cash Flow?

In business, cash flow is the amount of money flowing through a bank account. Your cash flow would be the amount of money you have coming your way, which might include …

✧ Job earnings after tax deductions (see Chapter 13, "You, the Law, and the IRS").

✧ Your allowance.

✧ Small business ventures (such as those mentioned in Chapter 17, "Mind Your Own Business").

✧ Investment dividends.

✧ Trust distributions.

Use the following worksheet to help you calculate your cash flow.

Your Weekly Cash Flow

Source of Income	Amount of Income
Paycheck	_____
Allowance	_____
Other	_____
_____	_____
_____	_____
Total income (cash flow):	_____

After entering all of your sources of income, estimate the amount of your income from each one on a weekly basis. Add up those amounts, and you've got the total of your weekly cash flow!

The Basics: What Do You Need?

The following worksheet is for you to list your most-needed items and how much they will cost you per week. Try to think of everything you will need to pay for during the week, including expenses such as birthday presents, work clothes, lunch money, and transportation.

Laser Pointer

One item that could appear on either or both of "Your Most Needed" worksheet and "Your Most Wanted" worksheet is savings. There may be something like college tuition (needed) or travel (wanted) that you're looking forward to in the future.

Your Most Needed

Need This Item	Cost	Priority
_____	_____	_____
_____	_____	_____
_____	_____	_____
_____	_____	_____
_____	_____	_____
_____	_____	_____

Total costs: _____

Your total cash flow: _____

Leftover cash flow: _____

Now that you've filled out "Your Most Needed" worksheet, do the following:

1. Enter your cash flow (from the "Your Most Needed" worksheet).

2. Prioritize the items according to how much you need each one (put "1" next to your most-needed item, "2" next to your second most needed, and so on).

3. Add up the total cost of your items in the cost column.

4. Subtract the total cost from your total cash flow to come up with your leftover cash flow.

Is your total cash flow big enough to cover the things you absolutely have to have? If you have more green than you need, move on to the next section to see what you can do with your extra money.

If you don't have enough to cover the things you need, look for ways to …

✧ Cut down on your needs by eliminating or reducing the amount of one or more of the items on your list.

✧ Earn more money (maybe work more hours at your job, take an additional job, or change jobs to one that pays more).

The Mosh Pit

Use a pencil instead of a pen to enter figures in "Your Most Wanted" worksheet and "Your Most Needed" worksheet. That way you can adjust the amounts without creating a mess.

You might be able to beef up your income by starting a small, part-time enterprise. Consider one of the small business ideas (like a yard sale) mentioned in Chapter 17.

The Extras: What Do You Want?

Now for the fun stuff: the things you want but don't absolutely need to buy. Here's "Your Most Wanted" worksheet.

Your Most Wanted

Want This Item	Cost	Priority
_____	_____	_____
_____	_____	_____
_____	_____	_____
_____	_____	_____
_____	_____	_____
_____	_____	_____

Total costs: _____

Your total cash flow: _____

Leftover cash flow (from "Your Most Needed" worksheet):

_____

Now that you've listed all the things you want, follow these steps:

1. Prioritize your items so that "1" is next to the item you want the most.

2. Write the total cost of your wanted items.

3. Enter the amount of leftover cash flow from "Your Most Needed" worksheet.

Do you have enough money in #3 to pay for everything on "Your Most Wanted" worksheet? If not, do one of the following:

✧ Cut back on the number of items you want, starting with the ones you want the least.

✧ Decrease the amount of money allotted for one or more of your items so that your total comes within your budget.

Cutting back on things you want isn't easy, but here are a few ways to do it without it hurting too much:

✧ Become a bargain hunter, tracking down the best deals through discount houses, Web sites, and mail-order catalogs for the exact items you want. For instance, you might find jeans sold online for 75 percent of the cost of the same jeans sold at a local department store.

✧ Settle for mid- or lower-range quality on stuff you buy. For example, maybe you could do with a stereo system that's a few hundred dollars less than a state-of-the-art system.

✧ Consider buying secondhand merchandise. More and more of your smart generation are hitting yard sales and consignment stores where they get great stuff for a fraction of the original price.

Keep juggling your figures until you come up with a perfect balance on "Your Most Wanted" worksheet. It's going to feel good to know that you can afford both the things that you need and want most.

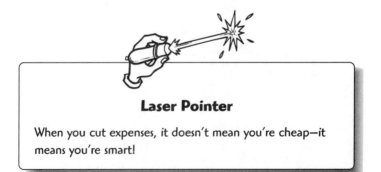

Laser Pointer

When you cut expenses, it doesn't mean you're cheap—it means you're smart!

The Least You Need to Know

❖ Developing good saving and spending habits will pay off down the line.

❖ Your cash flow is the total amount you get from allowance, your paycheck, and any other sources of income you might have.

❖ Make a list of all the things you absolutely need so you can figure out if you have enough cash flow to cover those expenses.

❖ Add up the costs of all the things you want to see if you can afford them with your cash flow.

❖ Remember to include savings in your list of needed or wanted items.

❖ Try to reduce your expenses or increase your income in order to create a plan that works for you.

Part 5

Outside the Job Box

You're an adventurer! You don't quite fit into the traditional job situation and you'd like to find an alternative. Maybe you want to give your time for free to an organization you believe in, perhaps you'd like to get an internship that supports an area of your studies, or maybe you want to be self-employed. If any one of these three is the case for you, you've opened the right part of this book.

The following chapters examine how to pursue volunteerism, internships, and self-employment. You'll learn how find and get going in each of these untraditional work roles.

Chapter 15

Volunteerism That Pays Off

In This Chapter

✧ Cherishing the spark of idealism within you

✧ Figuring out what concerns and interests make you want to volunteer

✧ Finding a position that uses your skills

✧ Applying for a volunteer job

You want to make a difference. You don't really need to make money during your time off, and you'd like to get involved in a cause that means something to you and the world around you. You want to volunteer.

This chapter will open the door to a number of volunteer opportunities, explain how to apply for them, and talk about what benefits you'll reap from doing work for free.

Idealism Is Good

Idealism is that tiny spark inside each of us that makes us believe that the world can be a better place if we kick in some personal resources. Resources needn't necessarily mean money. You can donate your time, talents, or physical strength—whatever it is that fills a need.

Idealism is what leads most volunteers to give anywhere from 1 to 40 hours a week to a cause they believe in. Volunteering has become a very popular pastime in recent years, especially among younger people. So when you become a volunteer, you won't be alone!

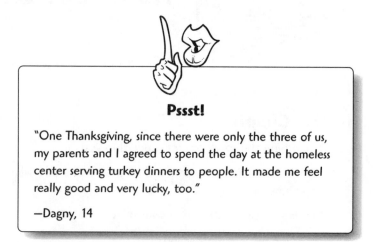

Pssst!

"One Thanksgiving, since there were only the three of us, my parents and I agreed to spend the day at the homeless center serving turkey dinners to people. It made me feel really good and very lucky, too."

—Dagny, 14

Why are you even thinking about donating your spare time for free? I can think of six good reasons. You'll ...

◇ Make a contribution toward a cause you believe in.

◇ Feel good inside.

◇ Learn new things.

◇ Meet new people with interests similar to yours.

◇ Gain skills and experience that will look great on job and college applications.

◇ Impress your friends and family.

Giving time to a cause is a strong statement about what you believe in. When you tell someone (a friend, date, or even an employer) that you volunteer for a particular group, you're giving them a big hint as to what your concerns and interests are. After all, you're doing it for *free!*

The Lay of Volunteerland

There are many causes to choose from when it comes to volunteering. Which of the following areas sparks your interest?

- ✧ **Social reform.** Maybe you get heated up over issues like politics, civil rights, or environmental hazards.

- ✧ **Education.** You might have a strong desire to promote educational issues such as literacy, mentoring kids, or library access.

- ✧ **Humanitarian.** Perhaps you'd like to do something to help people in need, such as the homeless, elderly, or disabled.

- ✧ **The arts.** Maybe you feel the community should support more performing and fine arts projects.

- ✧ **Religious or spiritual.** You might feel a need to give time to your church, synagogue, or spiritual community.

Inside Dope

For a list of international nonprofit organizations that offer volunteer positions, go to www.escapeartist.com/jobs35/jobs35.htm.

Maybe you lean toward more than one of these categories. In that case, find an organization that addresses both of them.

For instance, if you're drawn to both humanitarian and educational causes, you could volunteer at an organization that educates first-time dog owners on how to train and care for their pets.

What Lights Your Fire?

To see what turns your particular spark into a flame, try taking this quiz.

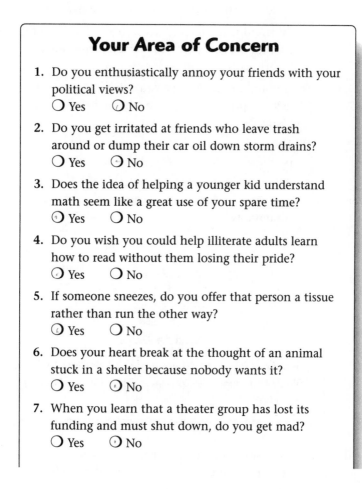

Your Area of Concern

1. Do you enthusiastically annoy your friends with your political views?
   ◯ Yes ⦿ No

2. Do you get irritated at friends who leave trash around or dump their car oil down storm drains?
   ◯ Yes ⦿ No

3. Does the idea of helping a younger kid understand math seem like a great use of your spare time?
   ⦿ Yes ◯ No

4. Do you wish you could help illiterate adults learn how to read without them losing their pride?
   ⦿ Yes ◯ No

5. If someone sneezes, do you offer that person a tissue rather than run the other way?
   ⦿ Yes ◯ No

6. Does your heart break at the thought of an animal stuck in a shelter because nobody wants it?
   ◯ Yes ⦿ No

7. When you learn that a theater group has lost its funding and must shut down, do you get mad?
   ◯ Yes ⦿ No

8. Do you believe that the community is better off with public art displays such as murals, exhibitions, and fine art in public buildings?
   ◯ Yes ⊘ No

9. Do you feel called by a higher power to do good?
   ⊘ Yes ◯ No

10. Would your community feel a loss if one of your church's or synagogue's charities didn't continue?
    ◯ Yes ⊘ No

Now, let's see how your "yes" answers could translate into areas of volunteerism.

1. **Social reform.** The political process might intrigue you. You may want to devote some time helping a campaign that fits in with your views.

2. **Social reform.** There are many environmental groups that might appeal to you. You could volunteer in the political arena or hook up with a group that physically attends to the issues (such as a water purification plant).

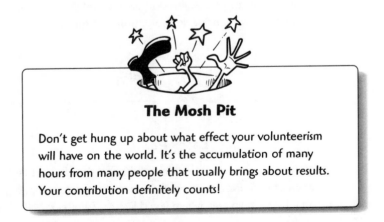

The Mosh Pit

Don't get hung up about what effect your volunteerism will have on the world. It's the accumulation of many hours from many people that usually brings about results. Your contribution definitely counts!

3. **Education.** There's a lot of fertile ground out there for your volunteerism—all communities have schools and most of them welcome help.

4. **Education.** You'll be happy to hear that there are literacy programs that teach adults while respecting their dignity.

5. **Humanitarian.** There are many care giving opportunities available to you. You could work in a senior citizens' center, nursing home, hospital, or convalescent home.

6. **Humanitarian.** Your love of animals could lead you to offer your time to an animal shelter, rescue mission, animal rights publication, or political organization that addresses these issues.

7. **The arts.** Your fiery spirit can be harnessed for the good by a political group dedicated to public funding of the arts.

8. **The arts.** You might enjoy volunteering for a group that does fundraising for the arts, or you could work directly with an art school, theater troupe, or children's art project.

9. **Religious or spiritual.** You're in luck—there are countless ways for you to respond to that call. You can do spiritual work in person, by phone, or online.

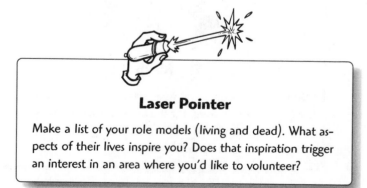

Laser Pointer

Make a list of your role models (living and dead). What aspects of their lives inspire you? Does that inspiration trigger an interest in an area where you'd like to volunteer?

10. **Religious or spiritual.** Most religious organizations have community projects that desperately need your help. If you pick one and give it your time, it stands a good chance of succeeding.

Finding Your Niche

You now have an idea of what type of organization you'd like to be involved with. But what exactly would you like to do within that organization? Read through the following list of volunteering options (organized by type of work) and see which ones appeal to you.

Office Work

Receptionist	Mail clerk
Administrative assistant	Messenger
Junior administrative assistant	Writer
Word processor	Proofreader
Data-entry keyer	Copy editor

Technical Projects

Web site developer	Technical support person
Computer programmer	Printing press operator

Teaching

Library assistant	Information booth
After-school program assistant	attendant
Medical and scientific illustrator	Docent

Care-Giving

Child-care worker	Veterinarian's assistant
Home companion	Kennel attendant
Candy striper	Dog and cat groomer

Food Operations

Cook	Kitchen helper
Baker	Busperson
Food server	

Inside Dope

For more lists of volunteer positions, job descriptions, and contact information in your area, conduct an Internet search using the words "volunteer jobs" and the name of your city or state.

Outdoor Work

Camp counselor	Dog walker
Swimming instructor	Wildlife preserve worker
Lifeguard	Groundskeeper

Event Production

Event planner	Stagehand
Ticket taker	Costumer's helper
Usher	Stage set designer

Fundraising

Store salesperson	Telemarketer
Donation solicitor	Auction runner

Art Projects

Cartoonist	Graphic designer
Photographer	

Most of these job descriptions appear in Part 2, "Top Fifty Jobs." As you read each description, imagine doing the job for a nonprofit organization for free.

Putting Things Together

Now that you've figured out what type of work you want to do and what kind of organization you want to do it in, let's put those two pieces together in this worksheet:

Your Volunteer Job

Type of organization: _____

Kind of job: _____

Wasn't that easy? Now on to finding that volunteer op!

Where the Volunteer Ops Are

The need for community service is all around you. There's bound to be an organization that addresses your hot issue and that has an office in your part of the country. Check your Yellow Pages under the type of organization you're interested in to see what nonprofits are listed. If that doesn't give you good results, go on the Internet and see what volunteer activities exist there. (Yep, you could become a cyber volunteer!)

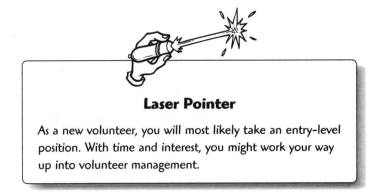

Laser Pointer

As a new volunteer, you will most likely take an entry-level position. With time and interest, you might work your way up into volunteer management.

VolunteerMatch (www.volunteermatch.org/results/index. jtmpl) is a Web site designed to link nonprofit organizations with those who want to help out. Its search engine allows you to see what organizations are "hiring" in your neck of the woods and what positions they're offering. Because these postings get updated frequently, check the site from time to time to get the latest info.

How to Become a Volunteer

All jobs, paid and unpaid, have certain requirements. Applying for a community service position is, in many ways, similar to applying for a paid position. You need to ...

⬥ Research the job to understand what it entails (see Part 2).

⬥ Check out the organization to know that it's reputable (see Chapter 2, "Your M.O. at Work").

⬥ Submit a resume and cover letter (see Chapters 9, "Resumes That Rock," and 10, "The Big Cover-Up"), if required.

⬥ Fill out an application form (see Chapter 11, "Blankety-Blank Applications").

⬥ Sit for an interview with a "hiring" manager (see Chapter 12, "Ace That Interview").

⬥ Formally accept the job and make agreed upon commitments.

Commitment is a key factor in being an effective volunteer. A good volunteer takes her position as seriously as she would take a paid job, because she understands that she's being counted on in much the same way that an employer counts on an employee to ...

⬥ Show up for work on time.

⬥ Dress appropriately.

⬥ Try to get along with co-workers.

⬥ Perform tasks to the best of their abilities.

When you find the right volunteer job for you, you'll know it by the way you feel. You'll look forward to doing it and you'll walk away from each session with a sense of reward. Sometimes that's something money can't buy.

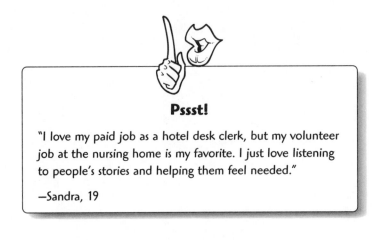

Pssst!

"I love my paid job as a hotel desk clerk, but my volunteer job at the nursing home is my favorite. I just love listening to people's stories and helping them feel needed."

—Sandra, 19

The Least You Need to Know

⬧ Because volunteerism doesn't involve pay, look for a volunteer position that will reward you emotionally, socially, and perhaps spiritually.

⬧ Find an organization that addresses an area of concern for you: perhaps social reform, education, humanitarian, the arts, or religious/spiritual.

⬧ Look for a volunteer job that suits your skills and interests within an organization whose cause you care about.

⬧ Apply for a volunteer position in much the same way you would apply for a paid job.

⬧ Once you land the volunteer position, commit yourself to it as seriously as you would commit to a paid position.

Chapter 16

Inside Internships

In This Chapter

◇ Understanding the difference between an internship and a typical job

◇ How an internship program benefits an employer and an intern

◇ What internships are out there

◇ How to go after an internship

Internships are on the rise, becoming more and more popular among employers and career-minded students. An internship isn't easy to win, but if you're lucky enough to get one, it could be incredibly valuable to your long-term planning.

If you're itching to be called an intern, this chapter is for you. It explains the difference between a regular job and an internship, and how to become an intern.

What Exactly Is an Internship?

An internship is a work experience that has a learning component built into it. An intern is a worker (frequently a student) who agrees to work for an employer who, in return, agrees to serve as the student's professional mentor.

How does an intern's job description read? Job descriptions vary, but almost all of them include these three tasks:

1. Assist in a particular project that's headed up by a knowledgeable professional and which is suited to the student's level of learning in that field

2. Conduct research (otherwise known as fact finding)

3. Provide support (typing, filing, errands, and other grunt work)

Pssst!

"I was an intern at a biology lab that did cancer research. It was cool being part of all the experiments, but I really liked thinking that I was making a difference in how other people lived."

—Susan, 18

Although number 1 (working on a project) may seem like the most exciting feature of an internship, numbers 2 and 3 (conducting research and providing support) can be extremely valuable to an intern. Witnessing and being a part of the everyday operations can tell you a lot about a profession—and it may even tell you that a job in that field is really not your cup of tea.

Andy was an intern in a film production studio where he ran errands, answered phones, and did word processing. Although he hardly spent any time on the set, he knew after six weeks that such a fast-paced, competitive profession wasn't for him. He then went on to pursue a career in media research, which suited him far better.

What's the Deal?

The details of how internships are set up vary from employer to employer. Issues at stake include ...

✧ Will the intern be paid, work for free, or pay a fee to the employer for the privilege of interning? (Yes, in some cases, the employer expects the worker to pay!)

✧ How long will the internship be? It may last anywhere from a few weeks to several months; the duration will be agreed upon in advance.

✧ How much individual attention will the intern get? Some interns work side by side with leading experts in their field, while others work on teams that are visited occasionally by an expert.

These are all matters that you should investigate when you apply for an internship, and that you can ask about during your interview.

Looking at Both Sides

Internships are beneficial to both employers and interns. An employer likes hosting an internship program because it attracts workers who are ...

✧ Eager to learn and therefore easy to train in the company's style.

✧ Energetic.

✧ Willing to work for little or free.

✧ Possible candidates (who are already trained) for permanent positions in the company when the internship ends.

Inside Dope

Check out www.internjobs.com for an easy search of currently available internships, listed by state.

As a student, you can benefit from an internship because the program is likely to offer ...

✧ Insight into a possible career.

✧ Mentorship in a field you're eager to advance in.

✧ School credit (in some schools).

✧ Excellent credentials for college applications.

✧ Impressive experience to be listed on your resume (see Chapter 9, "Resumes That Rock").

✧ Future references that are well-regarded in the profession (see Chapters 1, "What's So Cool About Having a Job?" and 10, "The Big Cover-Up").

✧ An inside edge in getting hired and negotiating salary in your budding career down the road.

As you can see, the intern has a lot to gain, as does the employer.

What Type of Intern Are You?

You may already have an idea of the type of internship you'd like; you may even have a specific one in mind. If not, take a look at the following list, which categorizes internships according to the school subjects discussed in Chapter 2, "Your M.O. at Work."

Social Studies

Administrative intern

Advertising intern

Brand management intern

Business development intern

Business management intern

City host intern

Community outreach intern

Congressional intern

Customer service intern

E-marketing intern

Event marketing intern

General intern at the United Nations

Human resources intern

Investigative intern

Legislative and public policy intern

Marketing intern

Media research intern

Political intern

Public relations intern

Publicity intern

Real estate development intern

Sales intern

Tour guide intern

Inside Dope

Check out the current edition of *Internships* (published yearly by Peterson's Thomson Learning) for a listing of thousands of internships and employer contact information. This book is available at public libraries.

Science
Biology lab intern
Environmental intern
First aid intern

Research and development intern
Sanitation intern
Winery intern

Language Arts
Editorial intern
Interpreter intern

Magazine/newspaper intern
Technical writing intern

Math
Accounting intern
Accounts receivable intern
Architectural intern
Computer science intern

Insurance intern
Investment intern
Purchasing intern
Statistician intern

The Mosh Pit

Don't rule out an internship opportunity if it's not within a stone's throw from your home; see if the company provides housing for its interns and if you'd qualify for those accommodations. Rooming with a bunch of other interns could turn out to be a ton of fun!

Music and the Arts
Artist promotion intern
Film festival intern
Graphic artist intern
Artist intern
Music research intern

Photography intern
Record label intern
Stagehand intern
Storyboard art intern
Web site design intern

Laser Pointer

In some skilled professions, the learn-and-work job is called an apprenticeship instead of an internship.

Gym

Camp counselor intern

Outdoor education intern

Sports broadcast intern

Tech

3-D/animation intern

Carpenter's apprentice

Computer programming intern

Database administration intern

Electrician's apprentice

Film production intern

Graphics design intern

Hardware design intern

Help desk intern

Information systems intern

Multimedia intern

Online editor intern

Plumber's apprentice

TV production intern

Visual effects intern

Web site development intern

Some of these job titles are listed in Part 2, "Top Fifty Jobs," so check there to get their job descriptions. Others can be found on the Web (for instance, go to www.hoovers.com/career/dir, click on Job Search Sites, then click on Internships/Volunteer Opportunities) where internship descriptions are posted.

Make a Good Impression

Because internships are highly sought after by serious students, you'll need to be a strong candidate in the eyes of the employer to capture one. Here's what an employer is likely to look for in a candidate:

- ✧ School activities
- ✧ Related job experience
- ✧ Personal interests
- ✧ Volunteer experience
- ✧ Interpersonal skills
- ✧ Recommendations
- ✧ Availability (how many hours per week you can work)
- ✧ Majors in college or coursework in high school
- ✧ A winning attitude (the desire to succeed)

An employer may want to see your school transcripts in order to certify your grade point average. For some internship programs (such as in academic and scientific organizations), an employer may require that you have at least a 3.0 GPA.

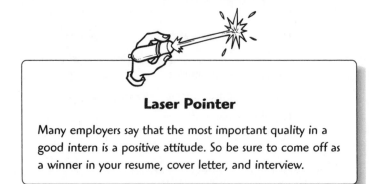

Laser Pointer

Many employers say that the most important quality in a good intern is a positive attitude. So be sure to come off as a winner in your resume, cover letter, and interview.

How to Apply for One

You've spotted the internship you want. Now what? Here's a step-by-step guide:

1. Get the hiring person's name, company name, address, and contact info of the place where you want to apply.

2. Do your homework to learn what the company's look-ing for in an intern applicant.

3. Get letters of recommendation (see Chapter 1).

4. Submit your resume, letter, and application form (see Chapters 9, 10, and 11, "Blankety-Blank Applications").

5. Get your school transcripts sent to the employer (if necessary).

Once you've completed these steps, you may have to sit back and wait a bit for a reply from the employer. Give it about two weeks, unless the internship posting says otherwise. If you haven't heard from the hiring manager by then, call her to see if she received your material and what the status of your application is. If all goes well, you'll be called in for an interview.

As I mentioned in Chapter 12, "Ace That Interview," spend some time before the interview creating a list of questions to ask during the interview. Your good questions will tell the employer that you're eager, inquisitive, intelligent, and on the ball—all qualities he's looking for in an intern.

Laser Pointer

Ask your school guidance counselor if he or she knows of any internships that might interest you. Counselors are often contacted by employers who want to be listed in the school's "available internship" files.

The Least You Need to Know

✧ Internships, or learn-and-work jobs, are becoming more and more popular.

✧ Internship programs can be found on the Internet, through your school guidance counselor, or by going directly to companies who offer such programs.

✧ Details like how the intern will be paid (or whether he will be paid) vary among employers; make sure you ask questions during the interview.

✧ One of the best advantages to landing an internship is the chance to find a great mentor who can help guide your career.

✧ Because internships are so sought after, you'll need to shine in your resume, cover letter, application, and at the interview.

Chapter 17

Mind Your Own Business

In This Chapter

✧ What it takes to be an entrepreneur

✧ Defining your idea of success

✧ Choosing a business that suits your skills and interests

✧ How to get your business up and running

✧ Dealing with business finances and government reporting

Does the idea of making a profit get your blood going? Do you like the thought of being your own boss? If so, maybe you should try your hand at running your own business.

If making things happen and taking full credit (and profit) is for you, you need to read this chapter. You'll learn about part-time and full-time businesses, how to choose one that suits your talents, and how to get it started.

The Entrepreneurial Fire

There's a certain fire in a successful entrepreneur. I'm not talking about someone having a high IQ, amazing inventions, or a ton of money (although none of these assets would be a bad thing to have on your side). I'm referring to the drive to succeed. Here's how most entrepreneurs demonstrate that drive. They ...

✧ Work long, hard hours at their businesses.

✧ Almost never stop thinking about how they can build their businesses.

✧ Regularly review their operations to see where they're doing well and where they need improvement.

✧ Network within their fields with eagerness to learn more about smart business strategies.

✧ Adhere to fair business practices.

✧ Strive to provide quality service or products.

✧ Feel proud to be the owner of even the smallest enterprise.

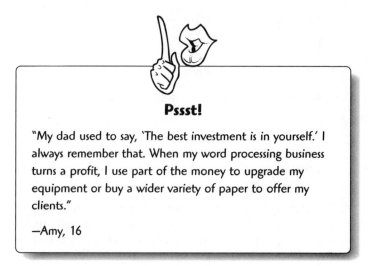

Pssst!

"My dad used to say, 'The best investment is in yourself.' I always remember that. When my word processing business turns a profit, I use part of the money to upgrade my equipment or buy a wider variety of paper to offer my clients."

—Amy, 16

That's a powerful package of professional traits that, when rolled up with a good business plan, can spell success.

Getting in the Groove

If you haven't already decided exactly what type of business you want to own, take some time now to browse through the following four business categories:

✧ **Care-giving.** This type of service involves taking care of people or animals in the areas of medical, educational, food, or safety needs.

✧ **Organizing/cleaning.** These businesses employ your organizational and cleaning skills to help customers get things done.

✧ **Technical/artistic.** This sort of service targets customers who need help with projects that require your technical or artistic skills.

✧ **Sales.** This type of business is one where you'd make money by selling stuff, either used or new.

Based on your skills, which of these categories suits you? To get a look at what businesses fall into each category, read on.

A Helping Hand

A business that offers help to people and animals can be extremely fulfilling to everyone involved. Here are some ideas that fit into this category. Just for the fun of it, I've suggested a name for each type of business:

✧ Dog walking service (Walking the Dog)

✧ Nonmedical care for the elderly, disabled, or ill in their homes (Tender Loving Home Care)

✧ Baby-sitting service (Yo Baby-Sittin')

✧ House-sitting service (Eye on Your House)

✧ Tutoring service (Tutoring Talents)

✧ Handyman or handywoman service (Mr. Fix-It)

✧ Hauling service (Haul It Away)

✧ Gift buying and delivery service (Gift Givers)

✧ Food delivery service representing one or more restaurants (On the Double Food-to-Go)

✧ Service that prepares, freezes, and delivers a week's worth of homemade dinners to individuals' homes (Gourmet Vu Frozen Dinners)

The Mosh Pit

If you're considering a food preparation, home care, or baby-sitting business, check with your state health and safety agencies to learn if credentials, bonding, or insurance are required to offer such a professional service.

What other ideas and business names can you come up with? Maybe you'd like to incorporate your own name into the title (for example, Dana's Dinners for a frozen-food delivery service).

Organizer/Cleaner Extraordinaire

If you love organizing and cleaning things, you could fill those needs for many people. Here are 10 ways to turn your love into cash:

✧ Party planner and event coordinator (It's a Party! Planner)

✧ Small catering service for parties, private dinners, and receptions (Catering to Good Taste)

✧ Grocery delivery service (The Grocery Getter)

✧ House-cleaning service (Miracle Maid)

✧ Car washing, waxing, and detailing service (Good Karma Car Wash)

✧ Door-to-door flyer distribution service (The Flying Flyer Distributor)

✧ Lawn, yard, and gardening service (Green Thumbs Up)

✧ Recyclable materials pickup service (Back to Earth Recycling)

✧ Morning telephone wake-up service (Good Morning Wake-Up Service)

✧ Home and commercial window washing service (Squeaky Clean Window Washing)

Do any of these names make you start making lists and organizing your business? If so, they may be the key to your first enterprise.

Techies and Artists

One of the following businesses might be for you if you have a natural artistic or technical talent. Let's see if any of them make your fingers or feet start tapping:

✧ Party disc jockey (The Dancing DJ)

✧ Professional photographer (A Picture Says It All)

✧ Web site designer and developer (Web Site Wizardry)

✧ Computer hardware or software consultant for installations, troubleshooting, and repairs (You Don't Have to Be a Nerd)

✧ Street curb house number painting service (What's Your Number?)

✧ Face painter (Cheek Charmers)

✧ Word processing service (Word for Word)

✧ Silk-screen service (Silk Screen Sensations)

✧ Sign painter (Plain and Fancy Sign Making)

✧ VCR programmer (Never Miss an Episode)

Inside Dope

Check out *Better Than a Lemonade Stand, Small Business Ideas for Kids* (published by Beyond Words Publishing, Inc., 1992), written by Daryl Bernstein when he was 15 years old. His book's Web page is www.beyondword.com/books/bls/html.

With your special technical and artistic abilities in mind, develop a business that pays you to do your magic.

Have I Got a Deal for You!

It takes a special type of person to be a good salesperson. Extroverts do very well in this field, as do those with a love of what they're selling. Here are some entrepreneurial ideas you might be interested in starting. Notice that only the first two have business names listed here because the rest are ones you would do without a name:

- ✧ Manage a concession cart that sells food items in a busy part of town (Wheel Concession).

- ✧ Develop and distribute coupon booklets that represent local merchants (Coupon Clippers).

- ✧ Door-to-door sales of a product you truly believe in.

- ✧ Deal in antiques. Buy inexpensive antiques at yard sales and resell them at antique auctions, flea markets, or antique malls.

- ✧ Use your artistic skill to make items (like jewelry, clothing, or leather goods) that can be sold to retail outlets.

✧ Organize yard sales (also called tag sales) to sell your own and other people's stuff.

✧ Sell your used garments through consignment shops.

✧ Resell your old audio- and videotapes, CDs, and DVDs through used record stores.

✧ Take your old books to used bookstores and sell them.

✧ Sell banner ads on your Web site and on others.

As you can see, you don't need a store front to have a sales business. You just need a product or service, some creativity, and a lot of stamina. If you've got all three, you've got it made!

Putting Out Your Shingle

Before you post signs around town about your new business, let's think through how you're going to start and run it.

Here's a 10-point plan to get your new venture up and going:

1. Decide what kind of business you want to have.

2. Research your competition to know what their services or products are like, how much they charge, and what type of people are their customers.

3. Come up with a clever name for your biz.

4. Develop a marketing plan for getting customers.

5. Figure out how much startup money you'll need to set up your operation and launch your marketing campaign. If you don't have enough cash, go back to square one and choose a business you can afford.

6. Investigate what governmental procedures need to be followed to become the owner of such a business (depending on what business you have, you may need a business license, health inspection, or other certification). Initiate that process.

7. Calculate what ongoing business expenses you'll have.

8. Decide what your prices will be and how many customers per week you'll need in order to make a profit.

9. Set a date to open up shop.

10. Launch your marketing campaign (#4) in time to get customers on opening day.

Laser Pointer

Get the support you need for starting a small business by asking for advice from a business professional you know and trust. Having an advisor is an excellent way to learn how to capture opportunities and avoid mistakes.

This plan might need to be adjusted, depending on what type of business you choose, who your customers are, and where you are in the country.

Taking Care of Business

There's no question that profit is important—without it a business can't stay afloat. So let's look at what it means for a business to be profitable.

The formula is very simple: R – E = P (Revenue minus Expenses equals Profit). That being the case, there are two ways to develop profit:

1. Increase your revenue (the amount of money you have coming in)

2. Decrease your expenses (the amount of money you have going out)

The Mosh Pit

To avoid a lot of financial pressure, start out small and build your business gradually. That way you can learn as you go without feeling that your whole bank account is at big risk.

Here's a worksheet to keep track of these two activities:

Your Weekly Revenue

Source of Income	Amount
1. _____	_____
2. _____	_____
3. _____	_____
4. _____	_____
5. _____	_____
6. _____	_____
7. _____	_____
8. _____	_____
9. _____	_____
10. _____	_____

Total weekly revenue: _____

Your Weekly Expenses

Item	Cost
1. _____	_____
2. _____	_____
3. _____	_____
4. _____	_____
5. _____	_____
6. _____	_____
7. _____	_____
8. _____	_____
9. _____	_____
10. _____	_____

Total weekly expenses: _____

Your Weekly Profit

1. Total weekly revenue: _____

2. Total weekly expenses: _____

3. Your weekly profit (line 1 minus line 2): _____

If "Your Weekly Profit" worksheet shows little or no profit, you need to increase your revenue, decrease your expenses, or do both. Here are tips on how to do each of those two things.

Bringin' in the Dough

Knowing how to increase revenue is key. Depending on what type of business you have, one or more of the following methods could do the trick:

✦ Launch an intensive marketing campaign. Create a sign, make phone calls to everyone in your personal network, or distribute tons of flyers, e-mail, direct mail, or discount coupons to potential customers.

✧ Work longer hours. The more customers you have per day, the more money you'll take in.

✧ Change your prices. Consider the effects of higher and lower rates: Would lower rates draw a larger volume of customers and generate greater revenue? Would higher rates increase your income even if the rates discouraged the number of sales?

Look at each figure on "Your Weekly Revenue" worksheet and ask yourself if there's any way to increase it. With a little creativity, you can come up with some good solutions.

The Mosh Pit

Before you get too excited about how much profit you're making, remember that you'll need to pay taxes out of that profit. To calculate how much will go to taxes, read Chapter 13, "You, the Law, and the IRS," and consult a tax preparer or your government tax agencies (see Appendix A, "Agencies That Work").

Cutting Costs

The other half of the equation is keeping your business expenses down. Here are some ideas for cutting your costs:

✧ Begin your business with just a few tools or pieces of equipment, enough to do a good job without all the bells and whistles. For example, use a push lawnmower in your yard maintenance service for a few weeks until you see that you have enough customers to justify buying a power mower.

✧ Use grassroots marketing instead of expensive advertising. For instance, advertise your baby-sitting service by distributing flyers door to door in your neighborhood instead of buying an ad in the newspaper.

✧ Offer unusually excellent products or services that will develop repeat and referral business at no marketing expense to you. For example, if the donuts at your concession stand are the best in town, you'll get a loyal following through word of mouth in no time.

✧ Don't hire anyone in your business until you absolutely have to. For instance, don't hire your sister Sunny to help call customers for your morning wake-up service until you have so many customers that you can't fill all the orders without her help.

✧ Buy your supplies at discount houses instead of regular retail stores. For example, buy the doggie treats for your dog-walking service at K Mart instead of that fancy pet supply store down the street.

✧ Don't buy more inventory than you need. In other words, until you know how many paper towels you'll go through per day in your window cleaning service, buy a six-pack instead of a case.

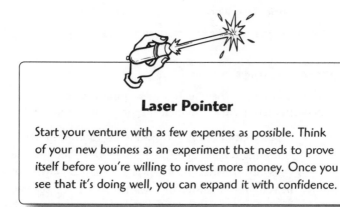

Laser Pointer

Start your venture with as few expenses as possible. Think of your new business as an experiment that needs to prove itself before you're willing to invest more money. Once you see that it's doing well, you can expand it with confidence.

Using these revenue and expense tips, keep tweaking the figures in your financial worksheets (and your business) until you get the kind of profit that spells success for you.

Keeping It Straight with the Government

Registering your business and reporting your income to your federal, state, and local governments may be important. Check with your local Chamber of Commerce and your state or county small business bureau to understand what's required of business owners. You may find that an operation as small as yours doesn't need to be registered in your area; or you may learn that you need to fill out a few forms and pay a fee. It all depends on ...

✧ What type of business you have.

✧ Whether or not you have employees.

✧ How much money you make.

✧ The relevant self-employment laws in your neck of the woods.

You'll also need to check with a tax professional (or your state tax board and the Internal Revenue Service) to learn how to report your income, how often to pay your taxes, and all that stuff.

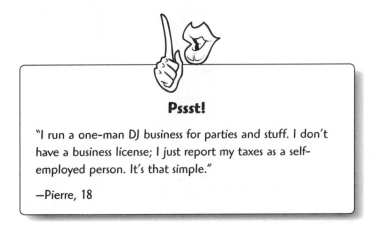

Pssst!

"I run a one-man DJ business for parties and stuff. I don't have a business license; I just report my taxes as a self-employed person. It's that simple."

—Pierre, 18

The Least You Need to Know

✧ Although being your own boss is a lot of work, there can be great psychological and financial rewards.

✧ Choose a business that uses either your care-giving, organizing/cleaning, technical/artistic, or sales skills.

✧ Develop a step-by-step financial, operational, and marketing plan for starting your business.

✧ Monitor your revenue and expenses on a weekly basis to know if you're making a profit.

✧ Be sure to file the appropriate business and tax forms with your local, state, and federal governments (if necessary).

Agencies That Work

Federal Department of Labor

The United States Department of Labor (DOL)
Washington, DC
200-219-5000
www.dol.gov

State Employment Agencies

The following list of government employment agencies is arranged by state or U.S. possession. Most have Web sites; others were still developing theirs at the time this book was published. If your state's employment agency Web site is not listed here, use a search engine to see if you can locate its Web address.

A list of links to all of the following Web sites can be found at www.nlma.org/lbrdepts.htm.

Alabama

Alabama Department of Labor
100 N. Union St., Suite 620
PO Box 303500
Montgomery, AL 36130-3500
Phone: 334-242-3460
Fax: 334-240-3417
www.dir.state.al.us

Alaska

Department of Labor
PO Box 21149
Juneau, AK 99802-1149
Phone: 907-465-2700
Fax: 907-465-2784
www.state.ak.us/local/
akpages/LABOR/home.htm

Arizona

State Labor Department
800 W. Washington St., Suite 403
PO Box 19070
Phoenix, AZ 85005-9070
Phone: 602-542-4515
Fax: 602-542-3104

Arizona Department
of Economic Security
Arizona One-Stop
Career Center
www.de.state.az.us/oscc

Arkansas

Department of Labor
10421 W. Markham
Little Rock, AR 72205
Phone: 501-682-4541
Fax: 501-682-4535
www.state.ar.us/labor

California

Department of Industrial
Relations
455 Golden Gate Ave., 10th Floor
San Francisco, CA 94102
Phone: 415-703-5050
Fax: 415-703-5059
www.dir.ca.gov

Colorado

Department of Labor and
Employment
2 Park Central, Suite 400
1515 Arapahoe St.
Denver, CO 80202-2117
Phone: 303-620-4701
Fax: 303-620-4714
cdle.state.co.us/default.asp

Connecticut

Labor Department
200 Folly Brook Blvd.
Wethersfield, CT
06109-1114
Phone: 860-263-6505
Fax: 860-263-6529
www.ctdol.state.ct.us

Delaware

Department of Labor
4425 N. Market St.,
4th Floor
Wilmington, DE 19802
Phone: 302-761-8000
Fax: 302-761-6621
www.delawareworks.com

District of Columbia

Department of Employ-
ment Services
Employment Security
Building
500 C St., N.W., Suite 600
Washington, DC 20001
Phone: 202-724-7100
Fax: 202-724-5683

Florida

Secretary
Department of Labor and
Employment Security
2012 Capitol Circle, S.E.
Hartman Building,
Suite 303
Tallahassee, FL 32399-2152
Phone: 850-922-7021
Fax: 904-488-8930
www.fdles.state.fl.us

Georgia

Department of Labor
Sussex Place, Room 600
148 International Blvd., N.E.
Atlanta, GA 30303
Phone: 404-656-3011
Fax: 404-656-2683
www.dol.state.ga.us

Guam

Department of Labor
Government of Guam
PO Box 9970
Tamuning, GU 96931-9970
Phone: 671-475-0101
Fax: 671-477-2988

Hawaii

Department of Labor and
Industrial Relations
830 Punchbowl St., Room 321
Honolulu, HI 96813
Phone: 808-586-8844
Fax: 808-586-9099
dlir.state.hi.us

Idaho

Department of Labor
317 W. Main St.
Boise, ID 83735-0001
Phone: 208-334-6110
Fax: 208-334-6430
www.labor.state.id.us

Illinois

Director
Department of Labor
160 N. LaSalle St., 13th Floor,
Suite C-1300
Chicago, IL 60601

Phone: 312-793-1808
Fax: 312-793-5257
www.state.il.us/agency/idol

Indiana

Department of Labor
402 W. Washington St.,
Room W195
Indianapolis, IN 46204-2739
Phone: 317-232-2378
Fax: 317-233-5381
www.state.in.us/labor

Iowa

Iowa Workforce Development
1000 E. Grand Ave.
Des Moines, IA 50319-0209
Phone: 515-281-5365
Fax: 515-281-4698
www.state.ia.us/iwd

Kansas

Department of Human
Resources
401 S.W. Topeka Blvd.
Topeka, KS 66603
Phone: 785-296-7474
Fax: 785-368-6294
www.hr.state.ks.us

Kentucky

Secretary
Labor Cabinet
1047 U.S. Hwy. 127 South,
Suite 4
Frankfort, KY 40601
Phone: 502-564-3070
Fax: 502-564-5387
www.state.ky.us/agencies/
labor/labrhome.htm

Louisiana

Department of Labor
PO Box 94094
Baton Rouge, LA 70804-9094
Phone: 225-342-3011
Fax: 225-342-3778
www.ldol.state.la.us

Maine

Department of Labor
20 Union St.
PO Box 259
Augusta, ME 04332-0259
Phone: 207-287-3788
Fax: 207-287-5292
www.mainecareercenter.com

Maryland

Department of Labor, Licensing
and Regulation
500 N. Calvert St., Suite 401
Baltimore, MD 21202
Phone: 410-230-6020,
ext. 1393
Fax: 410-333-0853 or
410-333-1229

Department of Labor, Licensing
and Regulation Commissioner
Division of Labor and Industry
1100 Eutaw St., 6th Floor
Baltimore, MD 21201
Phone: 410-767-2999
Fax: 410-767-2986

Massachusetts

Department of Labor and
Work Force Development
1 Ashburton Place, Room
1402
Boston, MA 02108
Phone: 617-727-6573
Fax: 617-727-1090

Michigan

Director
Department of Consumer
and Industry Services
PO Box 30004
Lansing, MI 48909
Phone: 517-373-7230
Fax: 517-373-2129

Minnesota

Department of Labor
and Industry
443 Lafayette Road
St. Paul, MN 55155
Phone: 651-296-2342
Fax: 651-282-5405
www.doli.state.mn.us

Mississippi

Workers' Compensation
Commission
1428 Lakeland Dr.
PO Box 5300
Jackson, MS 39296
Phone: 601-987-4258
Fax: 601-987-4233
www.mesc.state.ms.us

Missouri

Labor and Industrial Relations
Commission
PO Box 599
3315 W. Truman Blvd.
Jefferson City, MO 65102
Phone: 573-751-2461
Fax: 573-751-7806
www.dolir.state.mo.us

Montana

Department of Labor
and Industry
PO Box 1728
Helena, MT 59624-1728
Phone: 406-444-9091
Fax: 406-444-1394
dli.state.mt.us

Nebraska

Department of Labor
550 S. 16th St.
PO Box 94600
Lincoln, NE 68509-4600
Phone: 402-471-9792
Fax: 402-471-2318
www.dol.state.ne.us

Nevada

Labor Commission
555 E. Washington Ave., Suite
4100
Las Vegas, NV 89101
Phone: 702-486-2650
Fax: 702-486-2660
www.state.nv.us/busi_industry/
ir/index.htm

New Hampshire

Department of Labor
95 Pleasant St.
Concord, NH 03301
Phone: 603-271-3171
Fax: 603-271-6852
www.nhes.state.nh.us/
default.htm

New Jersey

New Jersey Department
of Labor
John Fitch Plaza
13th Floor, Suite D
PO Box CN 110
Trenton, NJ 08625-0110
Phone: 609-292-2323
Fax: 609-633-9271
www.state.nj.us/labor

New Mexico

Department of Labor
PO Box 1928
401 Broadway, N.E.
Albuquerque, NM
87103-1928
Phone: 505-841-8408
Fax: 505-841-8491
www.dol.state.nm.us

New York

Department of Labor
State Campus, Building 12
Albany, NY 12240
Phone: 518-457-2741
Fax: 518-457-6908

Department of Labor
345 Hudson St.
New York, NY 10014-0675
Phone: 212-352-6000
www.labor.state.ny.us/html

North Carolina

Department of Labor
4 W. Edenton St.
Raleigh, NC 27601-1092
Phone: 919-733-0360
Fax: 919-733-6197
www.dol.state.nc.us

North Dakota

Department of Labor
State Capitol Building
600 E. Blvd., Dept. 406
Bismarck, ND 58505-0340
Phone: 701-328-2660
Fax: 701-328-2031
www.state.nd.us/labor

Ohio

Bureau of Employment
Services
145 S. Front St.
Columbus, OH 43215
Phone: 614-466-2100
Fax: 614-466-5025
www.state.oh.us/obes

Oklahoma

Department of Labor
4001 N. Lincoln Blvd.
Oklahoma City, OK
73105-5212
Phone: 405-528-1500
Fax: 405-528-5751
www.state.ok.us/~okdol

Oregon

Bureau of Labor and
Industries
800 N.E. Oregon St., #32
Portland, OR 97232
Phone: 503-731-4070
Fax: 503-731-4103
www.emp.state.or.us

Pennsylvania

Department of Labor
and Industry
1700 Labor and Industry
Building
7th and Forster Sts.
Harrisburg, PA 17120
Phone: 717-787-3756
Fax: 717-787-8826
www.li.state.pa.us

Puerto Rico

Department of Labor and
Human Resources
Edificio Prudencio Rivera
Martinez
505 Munoz Rivera Ave.
G.PO Box 3088
Hato Rey, PR 00918
Phone: 787-754-2119 or
787-754-2120
Fax: 787-753-9550

Rhode Island

Department of Labor
610 Manton Ave.
Providence, RI 02909
Phone: 401-457-1701
Fax: 401-457-1769
www.det.state.ri.us

South Carolina

Dept. of Labor, Licensing and
Regulations
Koger Center, King St. Building
110 Center View Dr.
PO Box 11329
Columbia, SC 29211-1329
Phone: 803-896-4300
Fax: 803-896-4393
www.llr.state.sc.us

South Dakota

Department of Labor
700 Governors Dr.
Pierre, SD 57501-2291
Phone: 605-773-3101
Fax: 605-773-4211
www.state.sd.us/dol/dol.htm

Tennessee

Department of Labor
Andrew Johnson Tower
710 James Robertson Pky.,
2nd Floor
Nashville, TN 37243-0655
Phone: 615-741-2582
Fax: 615-741-5078
www.state.tn.us/labor-wfd

Texas

Texas Workforce Commission
101 E. 15th St., Room 618
Austin, TX 78778
Phone: 512-463-0735
Fax: 512-475-2321
www.tec.state.tx.us

Utah

Utah Labor Commission
General Administration
Building
PO Box 146600
Salt Lake City, UT
84114-6600
Phone: 801-530-6880
Fax: 801-530-6390
www.ind-com.state.ut.us

Vermont

Department of Labor and
Industry
National Life Building
Drawer #20
Montpelier, VT 05620-3401
Phone: 802-828-2288
Fax: 802-828-2195
www.state.vt.us/labind

Virgin Islands

Commissioner of Labor
Department of Labor
2303 Church St.,
Christiansted
St. Croix, VI 00820-4612
Phone: 340-773-1994,
ext. 230
Fax: 340-773-1858

Virginia

Dept. of Labor and Industry
Powers-Taylor Building
13 S. 13th
Richmond, VA 23219
Phone: 804-786-2377
Fax: 804-371-6524
www.vec.state.va.us

Washington

Department of Labor and
Industries
7273 Linderson Way
PO Box 44001
Olympia, WA 98504-4001
Phone: 360-902-4213
Fax: 360-902-4202
www.wa.gov/lni

West Virginia

Division of Labor
Bureau of Commerce
State Capitol Complex
Building #3, Room 319
Charleston, WV 25305
Phone: 304-558-7890
Fax: 304-558-3797
www.state.wv.us/bep

Wisconsin

Department of Workforce
Development
201 E. Washington Ave., #400 x
PO Box 7946
Madison, WI 53707-7946
Phone: 608-267-9692
Fax: 608-266-1784
www.dwd.state.wi.us

Wyoming

Department of Employment
Herschler Building, 2-East
122 W. 25th St.
Cheyenne, WY 82002
Phone: 307-777-7672
Fax: 307-777-5805
wydoe.state.wy.us

Cool Books and Web Sites

Job Search Books

The Back Door Guide to Short-Term Job Adventures: Internships, Extraordinary Experiences, Seasonal Jobs, Volunteering, Work Abroad, by Michael Landes; Ten Speed Press, 2000 (ISBN: 1580081479).

Better Than a Lemonade Stand, Small Business Ideas for Kids, by Daryl Bernstein; Beyond Words Publishing, Inc., 1992 (ISBN: 0941831752).

The Complete Idiot's Guide to the Perfect Cover Letter, by Susan Ireland; Alpha Books, 1997 (ISBN: 0028619609).

The Complete Idiot's Guide to the Perfect Resume, by Susan Ireland; Alpha Books, 2000 (ISBN: 0028610938).

How to Get a Job If You're a Teenager, 2nd Ed., by Cindy Pervola and Debby Hobgood; Alleyside Press, 2000 (ISBN: 1579500595).

The International Directory of Voluntary Work, by Louise Whetter and Victoria Pybus; Vacation-Work 1999 (ISBN: 1854582372).

Opportunities in Part-Time and Summer Jobs, by Adrian A. Pardis; VGM Career Horizons, 1998 (ISBN: 0844223166).

Peterson's Internships: The Largest Source of Internships Available (published yearly by Peterson's Thomson Learning).

Peterson's Summer Jobs for Students, Where the Jobs Are and How to Get Them (published yearly by Peterson's Thomson Learning).

Summer Opportunities for Kids and Teenagers (published yearly by Peterson's Thomson Learning).

Inspirational Books

Britney Spears' Heart to Heart, by Britney Spears and Lynn Spears; Crown Publishing Group, 2000 (ISBN: 0609807013).

Chicken Soup for the Teenage Soul III, Stories of Life, Love and Learning, written by teens; Health Communications, Inc., 2000 (ISBN: 1558747613).

Daily Reflections for Highly Effective Teens, by Sean Covey; Simon & Schuster Trade, 1999 (ISBN: 0684870606).

The 7 Best Things (Smart) Teens Do, by John C. Friel and Linda D. Friel; Health Communications, Inc., 2000 (ISBN: 155874777X).

The 7 Habits of Highly Effective Teens, The Ultimate Teenage Success Guide, by Sean Covey; Franklin Covey Company Inc., 1999 (ISBN: 1929494173).

Teen Ink, Our Voices, Our Visions, written by teens; Health Communications, Inc., 2000 (ISBN:1558748164).

Teenage Survival Manual, by H. Samm Coombs; Halo Books, 1998 (ISBN: 1879904187).

Job Hunt Web Sites

Damn Good Resume: www.damngood.com

Entry Level Job Seeker Assistant: www.dnaco.net/~dantassi/jobhome.html

gotajob.com: www.gotajob.com

InternJobs.com: www.internjobs.com

Internship Programs: www.internshipprograms.com/home.asp

Jobstar Summer Jobs: www.jobstar.org/adjobs/index.htm

OverseasJobs.com: www.overseasjobs.com

The Riley Guide Seasonal, Temporary, and Kinda Cool Work Options: www.dbm.com/jobguide/msc.html#summer

Seasonal and Summer Employment: dir.yahoo.com/Business_and_Economy/Employment_and_Work/Jobs/Seasonal_and_Summer_Employment/

SusanIreland.com: www.susanireland.com

SummerJobs.com: www.summerjobs.com

Summer Jobs for Teenagers: www.bygpub.com/books/tg2rw/summer-jobs.htm

U.S. Department of Labor Web site for Child Labor: www.dol.gov/dol/esa/public/youth/cltour1.htm

U.S. Bureau of Labor Statistics: stats.bls.gov/k12/html/edu_over.htm

Volunteer Jobs Overseas: www.escapeartist.com/jobs35/jobs35.htm

VolunteerMatch: www.volunteermatch.org/results/index.jtmpl

Other Cool Web Sites

Open Voice: www.pbs.org/merrow/trt/sites/openvoice.html

the nextSTEP: www.nextstepmagazine.com

PowerStudent: www.powerstudent.com

Student Center: www.studentcenter.org

Index

C

R